MANUFACTURERS OF AND DEALERS IN

MUSTARD, YEAST-POWDER, PEPPER-SAUCE, COFFEE, SPICES, SPLIT PEAS, &

ALSO,—COFFEE, SPICES, CREAM TARTAR, &c., GROUND AND PACKED TO ORDER AT SHORT NOTICE.

OFFICE, No. 8 CHATHAM ROW, BOSTON.

Bought of MAYNARD & CO.

Spices, Cream Tartar, s, &c.

50 MERCIAL STREET.

CHARLESTOWN STREET.

. F. CONANT,

N FOREIGN FRUIT,

REET, (Near Merchants' Row.)

R RAIL ROAD.

las Peirce & Co., in good order,

TER RAIL ROAD CORPORATION

and to be delivered to

r order the following Articles:

NUMBER OR WEIGHT.	MARKS

S Taft &
Worcester

Boston, Aug 16 185

Mess S Pierce & Co

Bought of EBENEZER NICKERSON & C

Wholesale and Retail Fish Dealers, No. 39 LONG WHARF.

TERMS CASH.

Boston June 18 186

Mess Silas Peirce & Co

LOAD CORPORATION,

To RUSSELL, FESSENDEN & WHITTEMORE,

MANUFACTURERS AND WHOLESALE DEALERS IN

SPICES, CREAM TARTAR, DRUGS, OAT MEAL &C., &

No. 52 Chatham Street.

TER, MANN & CO.

Bought of MARTIN L. HALL & CO

OLESALE GROCERS:

OLD BOSTON FARE

In Food & Pictures

OLD BOSTON FARE

In Food & Pictures

by Cynthia and Jerome Rubin

EMPORIUM PUBLICATIONS, S.A., Inc.

ACKNOWLEDGMENTS

We wish to thank all the many people who have enjoyed our past books and who have given us encouragement to write and research this one. Thanks are in order to Mary Lean of the Bostonian Society, Mr. Eugene of Eugene Galleries, Mr. Zepp of the Boston Public Library's Print Department, the librarians of the Charlestown Public Library, the Jacob Wirth Co. and, of course, Linda Bourke.

The Endpapers are a collage of old Boston invoices from food-related firms.

CREDITS FOR PHOTOGRAPHS

The Jacket Photograph is South Market Street in 1880. (Bostonian Society)

INTRODUCTION

The town of Boston was founded in 1630 by English colonists sent out by the "Governor and Company of the Massachusetts Bay in New England", under the leadership of John Winthrop, who arrived at Salem in June with the Charter of 1629. It originated in an order passed by the Court of Assistants in Charlestown, first selected as their place of settlement. But when the water proved unfit to drink, the colonists moved across the river to where Rev. William Blaxton, the pioneer white settler on the peninsula, lived on the highest hill's slope.

The Indian name was "Shawmutt" or "Shaumut" which signified "Living Waters" to some or "Near the Neck" to others. But the settlers called their community Boston after the English town many of them had left behind.

They laid out streets following the curves of the hills and built simple wooden houses along what later would become State Street and Dock Square. Governor Winthrop built his house on the future site of the Old South Meeting House,. His wife, like the other women in the town, baked her own bread and carried her pail to fill with water from the fresh spring that named Spring Lane.

The square where the Old State House now stands was the meeting place for business and pleasure in the first century of colonial Boston. Close by were the stocks, the whipping post and pillory.

As expansion began, the North End became the seat of gentility. When the future birthplace of Paul Revere was erected in North Square in 1676, today Boston's oldest house, the town's best families were already living there. By the early 18th century, Boston was rapidly spreading. Church Steeples dominated the skyline while their bells called people to prayer meetings. As the Bunch of Grapes Tavern acquired a reputation as the best punch house in Boston, the upstart Blue Anchor became famous for its delicious pudding. The Boston Common, by this time planted with trees and marked with footpaths, brought out couples for a leisurely stroll following afternoon tea.

In the mid-1700's, Boston was prospering with its fishing fleets, ship building, importing and exporting. Later, the completion of Charles Bulfinch's new State House in 1798 marked the beginning of the development of Beacon Hill.

Whereas these early days were marked by abundant food, meals were plain but substantial. Often the family "dinner pot" contained boiled dinner to be topped off with Indian Pudding or dumplings. A cookbook was a treasured item to be cherished. It wasn't until 1796 that the first American cookbook was published in hartford, Connecticut by Amelia Simmons, an orphan. Although the English heritage was obvious, it was the first time recipes of purely American origin had been recorded. Many recipes characterized the plain, simple cookery which could be tasted on the Boston table. Here, out of tradition, was emerging a distinctive practical cuisine often learned from the Indians, and adapted to the New World.

From the Indians, New Englanders learned to tap maple trees and hence there is a long Boston tradition stemming from the introduction of maple syrup. Fortunate, indeed, had been the colonists who learned about corn; it was boiled on the cob, or cut off and cooked with shelled beans for succotash or dried and ground into meal for use the year round.

Local products, such as a variety of seafood, corn and cranberries, were accepted as well as the English background of puddings, pies and stewed dishes. The regional cookery had long become a stable factor in the Bostonian's way of life.

Favorite family dishes often became part of the weekly, seasonal or special occasion menus. Traditional dishes, such as boiled dinners, stews and chowders are still enjoyed, as well as roast turkey on Thanksgiving and salmon with peas on the Fourth of July. Boston cream pie, baked beans and brown bread are but a few of Boston's tempting legend.

We have long been fascinated with Boston's history and have compiled a good assortment of dishes along with some interesting tidbits of information and lore, which we have found more and more intriguing as we continue our research. For much of our historical knowledge, we have to thank Edwin Bacon, who wrote an endless number of guidebooks on Boston and first introduced us to the heritage we live with.

There were so many interesting old Boston photographs that we had to limit the number we chose, and, we think, you will find them as wonderful a documentary of Boston's immemorial charm as we do. These little glimpses into history are enchanting.

Tradition lives long in Boston. And we are fortunate to be able to sample many of the dishes which our forefathers ate. Because we have tried to make OLD BOSTON FARE a fine introduction to the best Boston has to offer, we hope you enjoy our efforts and the tradition that Boston has given us.

Cynthia and Jerome Rubin
Boston, Massachusetts

Oh! how my heart sighs for my own native land.
    Where potatoes, and squashes, and cucumbers grow;
Where cheer and good welcome are always at hand,
    And custards, and pumpkin pies smoke in a row;
Where pudding the visage of hunger serenes,
    And, what is far better, the *pot of baked beans*."
                    The New England Farmer, 1829

APPLE COBBLER

1 cup flour, sifted
2 tablespoons sugar
1½ teaspoons baking powder
¼ teaspoon salt
4 tablespoons butter
¼ cup milk
1 egg, slightly beaten
1 cup sugar
2 tablespoons flour
½ teaspoon cinnamon
¼ teaspoon nutmeg
6 cups apples, pared and sliced
1 tablespoon butter

Sift together the flour, 2 tablespoons sugar, baking powder and salt. Cut in the 4 tablespoons butter until mixture is coarse. Combine milk and egg. Add to the dry ingredients, stirring just to moisten. Set aside. For filling, combine the 1 cup sugar, flour, cinnamon, nutmeg and apples. Cook and stir over medium heat until tender, about 8 minutes. Pour into 8-inch round baking dish; dot with 1 tablespoon butter. Bake in 400° oven for 20 minutes. Serve warm.
(Makes 6 servings)

APPLE DUMPLINGS

2¼ cups flour, sifted
7-8 tablespoons ice water
½ cup sugar
¾ teaspoon salt
6 medium apples, pared
1½ teaspoons cinnamon
1 tablespoon butter

Sift flour and salt into mixing bowl. Add most of the shortening and cut with a blender until mixture looks like meal. Then add remaining shortening until mixture looks the size of giant peas. Sprinkle water lightly over mixture, blending until mixture can be pressed together into a ball. Roll out dough ¼-inch thick on a lightly-floured board. Cut in 7-inch piece squares. Pare and core the apples and place in pastry squares. Fill cavity of each apple with the sugar and cinnamon mixture. Dot with butter. Moisten points of pastry square and bring opposite points up over apple, overlapping them. Seal well. Place about 2-inches apart in 8 x 12-inch baking pan. Chill thoroughly in refrigerator.

SYRUP
1 cup sugar
4 tablespoons butter
¼ teaspoon cinnamon
2 cups water
Mix in pan, the sugar, cinnamon, butter and water. Boil 3 minutes. Pour hot syrup around the chilled dumplings in baking pan. Bake 5 to 7 minutes in a 500° oven. Reduce temperature to 350° and finish baking for 30 to 35 minutes. Serve warm with cream, if desired.
(Makes 6 servings)

The first known apple orchard in New England was planted prior to 1630 by Rev. William Blackstone, Boston's first settler. It was located on the most westerly of the summits of "Trimountain", later known as West Hill. According to records, it was still bearing fruit in 1765.

Apple Woman On Boston Common

BOSTON CREAM PIE

The story goes that one woman got bored making the usual two-crust pie for her husband and decided to play a trick on him. She baked a cake in a pie pan, split the layers, put them together with a cooked custard filling and named it Boston Cream Pie, which isn't a pie at all. We don't know how her husband reacted but Bostonians have been enjoying the dish ever since.

½ cup butter or margarine
2½ cups cake flour, sifted
3 teaspoons baking powder
½ teaspoon salt
1½ cups sugar
¾ cup plus 2 tablespoons milk
1 teaspoon vanilla extract
2 eggs
Cream Filling
Confectioners' sugar

Cream butter to soften. Sift in flour, baking powder, salt and sugar. Add ¾ cup milk and vanilla; mix until dry ingredients are dampened. Then beat well until thoroughly mixed. Add eggs and remaining milk. Beat well. Pour into 2 9-inch layer-cake pans, lined on the bottom with paper. Bake in preheated moderate oven at 375° for 20 to 25 minutes. Turn out on cake racks and peel off paper. Cool. Put cream filling between the layers and sprinkle top with confectioners' sugar.

CREAM FILLING

½ cup sugar
2½ tablespoons cornstarch
¼ teaspoon salt
1½ cups milk
2 egg yolks, beaten
1 teaspoon vanilla extract

In heavy saucepan mix sugar, cornstarch, and salt. Add ½ cup milk, and stir until smooth. Add remaining milk, and cook over low heat, stirring constantly, until smooth and thickened. Stir mixture into egg yolks. Put back in saucepan, and cook for 2 minutes longer, stirring constantly. Cool, and add vanilla.

Crowd In Downtown Street

OLD-FASHIONED MINCEMEAT

2 quarts apples
1 pound seeded raisins
2 pounds brown sugar
Juice of 2 lemons
1 teaspoon salt
1 teaspoon clove, ground
1 teaspoon nutmeg, ground
2 pounds stew beef
½ pound beef suet
1 pint meat liquid (broth water left from cooked meat)
1 teaspoon cinnamon
1 teaspoon allspice

Place stew beef into pan with 2 cups water. Cook slowly until meat is tender. Peel and slice two quarts of apples. Put apples, meat, raisins, and suet through food chopper. Add brown sugar, meat liquid, lemon juice, salt and spices. Mix well. Cook over low heat until mixture is cooked thoroughly, about 2 hours. Stir frequently. Seal in hot sterilized jars.
(Makes 6 quarts)

TOMATO MINCEMEAT

12 green tomatoes, peeled
9 large apples, peeled and cored
6 large pears, peeled and cored
3 large oranges, peeled and seeded
3 lemons, halved and seeded
7½ cups seedless raisins
1 cup brown sugar, packed
3 cups dark corn syrup or light molasses
1 cup cider vinegar
⅓ cup orange juice
⅓ cup lemon juice
2 tablespoons cinnamon
1½ teaspoons nutmeg, ground
1½ teaspoons cloves, ground
1½ teaspoons ginger, ground
1½ teaspoons allspice, ground
1½ teaspoons salt

Grind tomatoes, apples, pears, oranges and lemons well. Combine with raisins, sugar, corn syrup, vinegar and juices in a heavy kettle or pan. Heat to boiling. Simmer, stirring often, until mixture thickens, about 30 minutes. Add spices, and simmer 5 minutes. Seal in hot sterilized jars.
(Makes 12 pounds)

Tremont House Interior

BOSTON LOBSTER PIE

2 tablespoon butter
½ pound lobster, (1 well-packed cup)
¼ cup sherry
3 tablespoon butter
a little salt
1 tablespoon flour
¾ cup light cream
2 egg yolks, well beaten

Melt the 2 tablespoons butter; add sherry and boil one minute. Add lobster and allow to stand. Melt the 3 tablespoons of butter and add the flour, stirring mixture until it bubbles (about 1 minute). Remove from heat and slowly stir in cream and wine liquid drained from lobster. Mix egg yolks with small amount of sauce and gradually stir in remaining sauce. Cook over hot, but not boiling, water, stirring constantly until sauce is smooth and thick, about 3 minutes. Add lobster and turn into shallow caserole. Sprinkle with topping and bake in 300° oven for 10 minutes, or until browned.

TOPPING
¼ cup cracker meal
¼ teaspoon paprika
1 tablespoon potato chips, finely crushed
1½ teaspoons Parmesan cheese
2 tablespoons butter, melted
2 to 4 tablespoons sherry
(Makes 3-4 servings)

KEDGEREE

This recipe was brought home by seamen who sailed the clipper ships all over the world. New England homemakers substituted fish for the lamb called for in the original recipe. Eggplant was also an ingredient in the original recipe; New England homemakers used eggs thinking they were similar and came up with their own special Kedgeree.

2 cups hot cooked rice
2 cups flaked cooked fish
4 eggs, hard-boiled and chopped
3 tablespoons parsley, minced
¼ teaspoon thyme
½ cup heavy cream
Salt
Pepper to taste
6 rusks

Put the hot rice in the top of a double boiler. Add the flaked fish, chopped eggs, parsley, thyme, cream, salt and pepper. Stir gently to mix well. Place the rice mixture over boiling water and heat. Stir mixture gently. Serve rice mixture, at once, over rusks.
(Makes 6 servings)

Here were the headquarters for ships engaged in the China trade. Known, at one time, as "Brimmer's T", it was here that great cargoes of silk and tea were unloaded. Named T Wharf because it was T-shaped, many people make the mistake of connecting it with the Boston Tea Party which took place at Griffin's Wharf.

T Wharf, Boston Fish Pier

HUCKLEBERRY PUDDING

Well, now, said I, — suppose a good, clean wholesome-looking countryman's cart stops opposite my door. — Do I want any huckleberries? — If I do not, there are those that do. Thereupon my soft voiced handmaid bears out a large tin pan, and then the wholesome countryman, heaping the peck-measure spreads his broad hands around its lower arc to confine the wild and frisky berries, and so they run nimbly along the narrowing channel until they tumble rustling down in a black cascade and tinkle on the resounding metal beneath. — I won't say that this rushing huckleberry hail-storm has not more music for me than the "Anvil Chorus."
(The Autocrat of the Breakfast Table by Oliver Wendell Holmes)

2 cups flour, sifted
4 teaspoons baking powder
2½ teaspoons sugar
½ teaspoon salt
2/3 cup milk
1 cup huckleberries
¾ cup sugar

Combine and sift flour, baking powder, 2½ teaspoons sugar and salt. Add milk. Roll out the dough into a square approximately ½-inch thick. In the center of the dough, place huckleberries which have been washed and sugared. Fold dough so that berries are still in center completely surrounded by dough. Tie in a white cloth or bag, allowing room for swelling. Place bag in steamer and steam 1 hour. Serve hot with Pudding Sauce.

PUDDING SAUCE
¾ cup sugar
Dash salt
1 tablespoon cornstarch
1 cup boiling water
1 tablespoon butter
½ teaspoon vanilla

Mix sugar, salt and cornstarch. Cook in boiling water until clear. Add butter and vanilla. Serve hot.
(Makes 5-6 servings)

Berries For Sale

NEW ENGLAND BOILED DINNER

4 pounds corned brisket of beef
½ pound salt pork
Cold water to cover meat
1 medium cabbage
3 small white turnips, pared and cut in half
6 small onions, peeled
6 medium potatoes, peeled and cut in half
6 carrots, peeled
6 small, cooked beets

Put meat into large stew pot and cover with cold water. Cover the pot and bring to boil. Reduce heat and cook until beef is quite tender, about 2½ hours. Cut cabbage into 6 pieces and remove core. Add with turnips, onions, potatoes and carrots to meat. Cook until both meat and vegetables are tender, about 1 hour. Serve on a large platter with meat surrounded by vegetables. Heat beets just before serving and use for garnish.
(Makes 4-6 servings)

BEAN POT BEEF STEW

2 pounds stewing beef, chuck or round
Flour
3 tablespoons fat or cooking oil
1 medium onion, sliced
Hot water
1½ teaspoons salt
¼ teaspoon pepper
4 carrots, peeled and diced
2 small white turnips, pared and sliced
2 cups fresh peas
8 medium potatoes, quartered

Cut the meat into 1-inch cubes; coat with flour. Melt the fat in a skillet over medium heat. Add the meat and brown well on all sides; remove meat as it browns and place it in a bean pot. Preheat oven at 350°. Add the onion to the fat in the skillet; cook, stirring frequently, until golden. Put the onion into the bean pot. Pour enough hot water into the pot to cover the meat and onions. Add the salt and pepper. Cover the bean pot and bake 2 hours. Remove bean pot from oven. Add carrots and remaining ingredients. Pour in enough hot water to cover vegetables, if necessary. Cover and return bean pot to oven and bake 2 to 3 hours more or until meat and vegetables are tender.
(Makes 6-8 servings)

Cattle Market

STEAMED PUDDING

2 cups beef suet, chopped fine
2 cups bread crumbs
3 cups flour, sifted
½ cup brown sugar
1 cup fruit preserve,
  cherry, pear, or plum
2 pounds raisins
1 pound currants
½ pound citron, chopped
2 eggs, slightly beaten
1 teaspoon cinnamon, ground
½ teaspoon cloves, ground
½ teaspoon mace, ground
1 teaspoon baking powder
1 teaspoon soda
1 teaspoon salt
6 large apples, chopped fine
1 large orange, chopped fine

Put suet, apples, orange, and citron through food chopper. Add salt, soda, baking powder and spices to flour, then mix everything in a large bowl together. The syrup from the preserves with the juice from the apples and orange should make enough moisture for the batter. It should be about as thick as fruit cake. If batter is too stiff; add a little mild molasses or syrup. Fill 4 well-buttered pound coffee cans, ¾ full. Cover with lid buttered on inside. Place in hot water and steam 2 to 3 hours. Keep in a cool place, and reheat as needed. Serve with hard sauce.

HARD SAUCE
1 cup confectioners' sugar
⅓ cup butter
¼ cup wine
Nutmeg
Cream butter and add the sugar slowly, stirring constantly. Add wine, drop by drop and beat well. Sprinkle with nutmeg.
(Makes 6-8 servings)

BLUEBERRY GRUNT

2 cups fresh blueberries
1 cup water
½ cup sugar
¼ teaspoon cinnamon
1 cup flour
1¼ teaspoon baking powder
¼ teaspoon salt
2 tablespoons sugar
1 egg, well beaten
¼ cup milk
Cream, optional

Wash and pick over blueberries. Put water in large, heavy skillet; add 1 cup sugar and bring to a boil. Reduce heat; add berries and cinnamon and let simmer while preparing the rest. Sift dry ingredients into mixing bowl. Combine egg and milk and add to dry ingredients. Stir just enough to moisten. Drop dough by large spoonfuls on the boiling berries. Allow space between drops for dumplings to expand. Cook uncovered for 10 minutes. Cover skillet and cook 10 minutes longer. Serve warm with cream, or whipped cream.
(Makes 6-8 servings)

Charlestown Bridge And Elevated

BOSTON TEA

The Dutch East India Company introduced tea into the Netherlands early in the seventeenth century. It reached England as early as 1657 and was shipped by the English to the American colonies in 1680. At that time is was selling at five dollars a pound and upwards, according to the quality. At first tea was not favorably received. Its use was condemned by writers, educators, and clergymen as a heathenish and immoral practice. In England especially the drinking of tea was bitterly attacked.

Boston Tea is a cold weather beverage taken in a mug or porcelain cup whose size is related to weather conditions. Above freezing, 4 to 6 oz. is appropriate; a Northeaster rates 6 to 7 oz.; and if mittens must be worn, a large cup of 8 oz. capacity is convenient. In addition to conventional sweetners, the drink is reinforced with Apple Jack, a liquid sweetner sold under various tax stamps and recognized for its medicinal value by experienced cold weather hands. (*Old Almanac*)

LEMON TEACAKE

½ cup butter
1 cup sugar
2 eggs
1½ cups flour
1 teaspoon baking powder
½ teaspoon salt
½ cup milk
Juice of 1 lemon
½ cup sugar

Cream butter and 1 cup sugar; add eggs, and then dry ingredients alternately with milk. Grease and line a loaf pan with paper. Pour in batter and bake at 375° for about 50 minutes. When done, spread immediately with mixture of lemon juice and ½ cup sugar. Cool.

Miss Preble's Lunch And Tea Rooms

RAISIN DISCS

1 cup sugar
½ cup butter
2 eggs, beaten
1 teaspoon soda
½ cup milk
1 teaspoon cinnamon
½ teaspoon clove
¼ teaspoon nutmeg
1 cup raisins, chopped
3 cups flour, sifted
Sugar

Preheat oven at 400°. Butter cookie sheets. Sift flour, soda and spices. Cream sugar and butter; add well beaten eggs and beat vigorously. Add raisins and milk. Stir in flour. Dough should be stiff enough to roll easily. Add a very little more flour if needed. Roll quite thin. Cut with cookie cutter. Sprinkle with sugar and bake on prepared cookie sheet, about 12 minutes.
(Makes about 3 dozen)

CELERY SOUP

2 cups celery
1 quart cold water
2 slices onion
4 tablespoons butter
2 tablespoons flour
2 cups milk, scalded
1½ teaspoons salt
½ teaspoon mace
Cayenne
Celery salt

Chop celery; cook in water until tender. Cook onion and mace in milk 20 minutes; strain. Melt butter; add flour and seasonings. Combine celery and milk mixtures; thicken with butter and flour cooked together; cook five minutes and serve.
(Makes 6 servings)

CHEDDAR CHEESE SOUP

2 ounces butter
2 tablespoons whites of leek or mild onion
¼ cup carrots
¼ cup celery hearts or yellow heart leaves
1 lemon, grated rind
1 bay leaf
⅓ teaspoon dry mustard
1 quart rich chicken stock, boiling
6 ounces sharp Cheddar cheese, grated
1½ teaspoons Worcestershire sauce
Salt
Tabasco sacue

Melt butter in top of double boiler. Add leeks, carrots, celery and lemon rind and cook until transparent. Add bay leaf, pepper and mustard. Pour in stock and simmer for 20 minutes. Place pan over double boiler bottom that is filled with water just under the boiling point and whip in cheese. Combine 2 tablespoons of butter, 2 tablespoons of flour and 1 pint of hot milk into a cream sauce and whip into the mixture. Let stand 10 minutes. Strain this through cheesecloth. Add remaining seasonings.
(Makes 6 servings)

Faneuil Hall, "The Cradle of Liberty", was built in 1742 by Peter Faneuil, the Huguenot merchant, for a market and public hall and was presented to the town as a gift. Smibert, the pioneer painter, was the architect. It was rebuilt after a fire in 1763 and dedicated by James Otis. Bulfinch enlarged it in 1806. This was the scene of many a famous patriotic town-meeting, of the theatre of the British garrison, the town offices until 1822, the State dinners to Count d'Estaing, Lafayette and others as well as countless meetings on behalf of various movements addressed by Otis, Webster, Everett, Channing and other orators.

Originally called the Faneuil Hall Market, Quincy Market occupies the space between North and South Market Streets in front of Faneuil Hall. Built in 1825-1826 in the administration of the elder Mayor Quincy. Its architecture is of Quincy granite with four columns of Grecian Doric style at each end.

South Market Street

HERB DROPS

½ cup shortening
½ cup sugar
1 egg
½ cup molasses
2¼ cups flour, sifted
2 teaspoons baking soda
3½ teaspoons ginger
1¼ teaspoons cinnamon
½ teaspoon cloves
¼ teaspoon salt
⅓ cup hot strong coffee
2 tablespoons anise seed
2 teaspoons coriander seed, crushed
Walnut halves

Cream shortening and sugar together. Beat in egg and all molasses. Sift together flour, baking soda, ginger, cinnamon, cloves and salt. Add alternately to creamed mixture with coffee, mixing thoroughly. Stir in anise and coriander seeds. Drop from teaspoon onto greased cookie sheet about 2-inches apart. Bake at 350° for 8 to 10 minutes. Cool on rack and frost with vanilla glaze.

VANILLA GLAZE
2 cups confectioners' sugar, sifted
1 teaspoon vanilla
Milk
Combine sugar and vanilla. Add enough milk to make a spreading consistency. Top each cookie with walnut half.
(Makes about 40 cookies)

Herb Seller At Quincy Market

HERB BROILED FISH

⅓ cup butter, melted
1 tablespoon onion, grated
3 tablespoons lemon juice
1 teaspoon salt
½ teaspoon pepper
½ teaspoon marjoram or thyme
1 tablespoon chives
2 tablespoons parsley, chopped
4 6-ounce halibut, salmon
 or swordfish steaks

Prepare herb sauce by blending all ingredients except fish. Spread half the mixture on fish steaks. Broil for about 5 minutes. Turn steaks and spread with remaining sauce. Broil for 6 to 8 minutes longer, or until fish flakes easily.
(Makes 4 servings)

DINNER IN A DISH

4 tablespoons shortening
1 medium onion, chopped
2 green peppers, sliced
1 pound ground beef
1½ teaspoons salt
¼ teaspoon pepper
2 eggs
2 cups corn kernels
4 medium tomatoes, sliced
½ cup dry bread crumbs

Put shortening in a skillet and lightly fry onion and green pepper for 3 minutes. Add meat and blend thoroughly. Add seasonings; remove from heat, stir in eggs and mix well. Put 1 cup of corn in a baking dish, then half of the meat mixture, then a layer of sliced tomatoes. Repeat. Cover with crumbs and dot generously with butter. Bake at 375° for 35 minutes.
(Makes 4 servings)

FISH CHOWDER

3 pounds haddock fillets
Heads and tails of 2 fish
½ pound salt pork
8 medium potatoes, diced
6 medium onions, diced
1 quart milk
Salt
Pepper

Cover heads and tails with water; simmer 15 to 20 minutes. Cube salt pork and fry. When pork is brown, drain on paper, saving bits. Fry onions in pork fat until soft. Drain liquid from fish heads and tails into pan in which you will cook chowder. Cook potatoes in this liquid; add soft onions. Cut fillets into 2-inch squares. Add milk to potatoes, onions and liquid. Finally add fish. Heat thoroughly but do not boil. Season to taste.
(Makes 2 quarts)

Room At Crosby's, 19 School Street

VELVET MOLASSES KISSES

½ cup molasses
1½ cups sugar
½ cup water
1½ tablespoons vinegar
¼ teaspoon cream of tartar
4 tablespoons butter
¼ teaspoon baking soda
1 teaspoon vanilla or lemon extract

Put molasses, sugar, water and vinegar in saucepan. Stir until mixture boils; add cream of tartar. Boil until mixture becomes brittle when tried in cold water or to 256°. Stir constantly during last bit of cooking to prevent sticking. When nearly done, add butter and baking soda. Pour on buttered marble slab and when cool, pull until light colored. When pulling, flavor with vanilla or lemon extract. Cut into 1-inch pieces with scissors and wrap in wax paper.
(Makes about 25 pieces)
(*Adapted from an old recipe*)

YANKEE PRALINES

2 cups sugar
⅔ cup milk
1 cup maple syrup
1½ cups pecans, chopped

Boil sugar, milk and maple syrup until it forms a soft ball when dropped in cold water. Remove from fire and cool until lukewarm. Beat until creamy; add chopped nuts and drop from tip of spoon in small mounds on buttered paper.
(Makes about 25 pieces)

Copeland's Old Confectionery Shop

HAUNCH OF VENISON ROASTED

12 pound roast
4 cups flour
2 cups water
Salt, pepper and flour dredge
1 tablespoon currant jelly

Wipe meat carefully with wet cloth and cover with a large sheet of buttered paper. Make a thick paste of flour and water, roll out ¾ inch thick and lay over the fat side of the haunch. Cover with three or four sheets of white paper and tie securely with cord. Put in dripping pan and roast, basting frequently to prevent paper and string from burning. A twelve pound haunch will take 3 hours to roast. Half an hour before it is done, remove from the oven, cut strings, take off paste and paper; dredge with flour, salt and pepper; return to the oven and roast to a fine brown. Serve with a brown sauce to which a tablespoon of currant jelly has been added.
(*Adapted from an old recipe*)

RABBIT STEW

1 rabbit (3 to 4 pounds)
1 cup wine vinegar
1 cup onions, sliced
2 teaspoons salt
½ teaspoon cloves
¼ teaspoon thyme
¾ teaspoon red pepper sauce
1 cup flour
1 teaspoon salt
½ cup shortening
1 cup water
2 teaspoons sugar

Cut rabbit into serving pieces. Combine vinegar, onion, salt and seasonings. Marinate 5 hours. Strain reserve marinade. Combine flour and salt; coat the pieces of rabbit. Heat shortening in large skillet and fry rabbit until brown. Drain fat. Add marinade. Cover and simmer 45 minutes. Stir. Add sugar.
(Makes 4 servings)

PREPARING POULTRY
Pick, singe, and remove the crop, entrails, oil bag, legs, and pinions. Wipe, truss, dredge with salt, pepper, butter, and flour. Bake in a hot oven twenty minutes if liked rare, or thirty minutes if preferred well done. Serve with olive sauce and green peas. Geese and ducks have a strong flavor, and are improved by stuffing the craw and body with apples cored and quartered. The apples absorb the strong flavor, therefore should not be eaten. Celery and onions are also placed inside the duck, to improve its flavor.
(*Mrs. Lincoln's Boston Cookbook, 1884*)

Poultry And Game For Sale

CREAM OF OYSTER SOUP

1 quart oysters
1 tablespoon butter
1 tablespoon flour
½ pint cream, whipped
Salt
Pepper
Paprika

Scald the oysters in their own liquid; remove the oyster, chop and pound them in a mortar, then press as much as possible through a sieve. Make a mixture of the butter and flour; dilute with oyster juice. Add the oyster pulp, season with salt, pepper and paprika and keep hot until ready to serve. Just before serving add the whipped cream and beat it well into the soup.
(Makes 3-4 servings)

SATURDAY SPECIAL

1 cup pea beans
1 cup lima beans
1 cup kidney beans
1 cup yellow-eye beans
3 teaspoons dry mustard
3 teaspoons ginger
1 tablespoon salt
½ teaspoon pepper
½ pound salt pork
½ cup brown sugar
½ cup molasses or maple syrup
2 small onions

Pick over beans, wash, cover with water and soak overnight. Add salt and additional water to cover well. Bring slowly to boil. Simmer until skins of beans wrinkle when a few taken out on a spoon are blown upon. Drain. Save liquid. An old-fashioned bean pot is best but a covered casserole will do. Put ¼-inch slice of pork in the bottom of the pot, then alternate layers of beans with sprinkling of chopped onion until pot is two-thirds full. Score remainder of pork through the rind in ½-inch squares, ½-inch deep. Bury pork in top of beans with only the rind exposed. Heat liquid; add remaining ingredients and pour over beans, adding extra boiling water to the top level of beans. Cover; bake in a slow oven (225°-250°) for 6 or 7 hours. Uncover last hour.
(Makes 6 servings)

(*Adapted from an old recipe*)

The first "Marathon" to be run in America was held under the auspices of the Boston Athletic Association on April 19, 1897. The original course from Ashland to Exeter Street in Boston measured 25 miles and the first race finished with a lap around the Irvington Oval as part of a holiday tract meet.

The Boston Marathon

SNICKERDOODLES

New England cooks had a penchant for giving odd names to their dishes — apparently for no other reason than the fun of saying them. Snickerdoodles come from a tradition of this sort that includes Graham Jakes, Jolly Boys, Bramble Jambles and Kinkawoodles.

3¼ cups flour, sifted
½ teaspoon salt
1 teaspoon baking soda
1 teaspoon cinnamon
1 cup butter
1½ cups sugar
3 eggs, well beaten
1 cup walnuts, coarsely chopped
½ cup currants
½ cup raisins, chopped

Sift together flour, salt, baking soda, and cinnamon. Set aside. Work butter until creamy, then add sugar, a little at a time, beating until smooth. Beat in eggs thoroughly. Stir in flour combination, nuts, currants, and raisins. Drop from a teaspoon onto a greased cookie sheet about 1-inch apart, and bake in a preheated 350° oven for 12 to 14 minutes. Cookies keep well in an airtight container.
(Makes about 10 dozen cookies)

JOLLY BOYS

2 cups rye meal
1 cup flour, sifted
⅓ cup corn meal
¼ teaspoon salt
3 teaspoons baking powder
1 egg
1 tablespoon molasses
Cold water, about 1⅓ cups

Sift rye meal, flour, corn meal, salt and baking powder into mixing bowl. Beat egg and mix with molasses and 1 cup of water. Pour over dry ingredients and mix well. Add more water if needed to make a stiff batter. Cut batter from a tablespoon and fry in deep hot fat, that will color a one-inch cube of bread golden brown in 40 seconds at 385°. Cook to a rich brown.
(Makes about 10 dozen cookies)

(Adapted from an old recipe)

Between 1841 and 1851, various attempts at establishing a free public library had been made in Boston. After a while, a few books were donated; others had been exchanged with the city of Paris through Alexander Vallemore and Edward Everett gave his collection of U.S. public documents. He was named the first president of the board and it is to him that Boston citizens today are largely indebted for the successful organization of the enterprise.

Boylston Street Public Library And Hotel Pelham

MUSTER GINGERBREAD

Reminiscent of gala days of her youth when the Militia (M'lishee) gathered to be inspected and drilled. This yearly occurrence was known as 'Muster Day.' Hence the name — 'Muster Gingerbread'.
(*old lore*)

½ cup sugar
½ cup shortening (chicken fat preferred)
1 egg, beaten
1 cup molasses
3 cups cake flour, sifted
2 teaspoons soda
½ teaspoon salt
1 teaspoon ginger
1 teaspoon cinnamon
½ teaspoon nutmeg
¼ teaspoon cloves
1 cup boiling hot water

Preheat oven to 350°. Butter and flour two 10 x 7-inch, pans, or 8-inch square if thicker loaf is desired. Mix and sift flour, soda, salt and spices. Cream shortening and sugar. Add molasses and beaten egg. Stir in dry ingredients. Slowly add boiling water. Turn into prepared pans. Bake about 30 minutes until loaves are slightly and evenly rounded, not cracked open.
(Makes 2 loaves)

SOUR CREAM GINGERBREAD

½ cup sugar
½ teaspoon ginger
½ teaspoon salt
1 teaspoon cinnamon
2 teaspoons baking soda
1 cup molasses
1 cup thick sour cream
2 cups flour, sifted
1 egg

Combine sugar, ginger, cinnamon and salt in mixing bowl. Add sour cream. Stir baking soda into molasses. Stir in flour, mixing well. Add well beaten egg. Turn into buttered 8-inch square pan. Bake in slow oven at 325° about 45 minutes.

The Star Theatre, Tremont Row, 1912

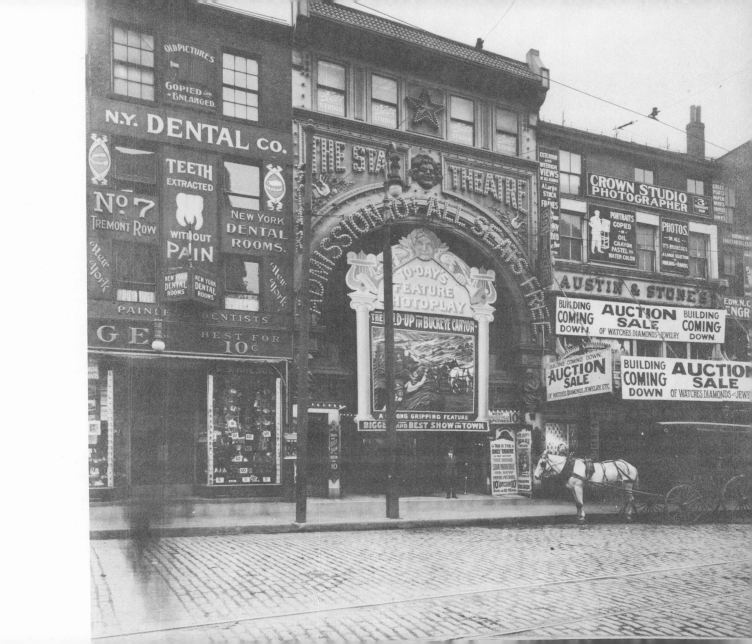

LAMB STEW

2 pounds lamb shoulder, boned
3 tablspoons fat
6 small carrots, peeled
1 large onion, chopped
¼ cup celery, diced
6 small potatoes, pared
1 white turnip, pared and sliced
1 teaspoon salt
¼ teaspoon pepper
1 bay leaf
Pinch sage
Water

Cut the lamb into 2-inch cubes. Heat the fat in a large heavy saucepan over medium heat. Add the lamb and brown well on all sides. Put the carrots, onion, celery, potatoes and turnip into the sauce pan with the lamb. Add and stir in the salt, pepper, bay leaf and sage. Pour enough water into the sauce pan to cover the meat and vegetables. Bring water to a boil; reduce heat and simmer, covered, 2 hours or until meat and vegetables are tender. Thicken stew with flour, if desired. Remove bay leaf. Serve with hot Johnnycakes, p. 68.
(Makes 6 servings)

RED FLANNEL HASH

1½ tablespoons butter or margarine
1 cup cooked corned beef, chopped
1 cup cooked beets, chopped
1 small onion, chopped
2 tablespoons cream
Salt and pepper to taste

Heat the butter in a large heavy skillet over medium heat. Combine the corned beef, beets, potatoes, onion and cream; season the mixture with salt and pepper. Spread corned beef mixture over the bottom of the skillet. Heat mixture slowly. When a brown crust forms on the bottom, crease across th center with a spatula and turn half the mixture over omelet-style and serve.
(Makes 4 servings)

Boston Note: Purists never grind the meat. Ingredients are chopped separately by hand in a wooden bowl.

Shopping District

ANADAMA BREAD

The story goes that Anadama bread was invented in the 1800's when a fisherman became enraged with his wife. All she would feed him would be corn meal and molasses. One night he had eaten it once too often and, enraged, he tossed flour and yeast into the corn meal and molasses and baked it. Later, while eating a bread that had no name he was heard to mumble over and over, "Anna, damn her!".

½ cup yellow corn meal
2 cups boiling water
2 tablespoons shortening
½ cup molasses
1½ teaspoons salt
2 packages active dry yeast
½ cup warm water, (not hot)
6 cups flour, sifted

Slowly add and stir the corn meal into the rapidly boiling water. Remove from heat; add the shortening, molasses and salt and stir until blended. Set the mixture aside until has cooled to lukewarm. Dissolve the yeast in the warm water according to directions. Add to the lukewarm corn meal mixture and stir well. Turn mixture into a large bowl. Add 3 cups of the flour and stir vigorously. Add enough of the remaining flour to make a stiff dough. Turn out the dough on a lightly floured board and knead until it is elastic. Grease a bowl well. Place the dough in the bowl and cover it with a dampened cloth. Let rise in a warm place, about 45 minutes, away from drafts or until it has doubled in bulk. Grease two 9 x 5-inch pans. Punch down the dough; turn it out on a lightly floured board and knead it for a few minutes. Divide the dough in half; shape each into a loaf. Place the dough in the prepared pans. Cover the pans with a dampened cloth and let rise in a warm place about 45 minutes or until doubled in bulk. Bake at 375° for 1 hour, or until browned.
(Makes 2 loaves)

BREAD AND BREAD MAKING

Importance of Bread. — Bread is one of the earliest, the most generally used, and the most important forms of food adopted by mankind. Nothing in the whole range of domestic life more affects the health and happiness of the of the family than the quality of its daily bread. With good bread, the plainest meal is a feast in itself; without it, the most elaborately prepared and elegantly served menu is unsatisfactory.
Bread-making is at once the easiest and the most difficult branch of culinary science, — easy, if only sufficient interest be taken to master a few elementary principles and to follow them always, using the judgment of the best authorities, until experience furnishes a sufficient guide; difficult, if there be any neglect to use proper care and materials. It should be regarded as one of the highest accomplishments; and if one tenth part of the interest time, and thought which are devoted to cake and pastry and fancy cooking were spent upon this most important article of food, the presence of good bread upon our tables would be invariably secured. (Mrs. Lincoln's Boston Cookbook, 1884)

Mary J. Lincoln, Noted Boston Cookbook Author

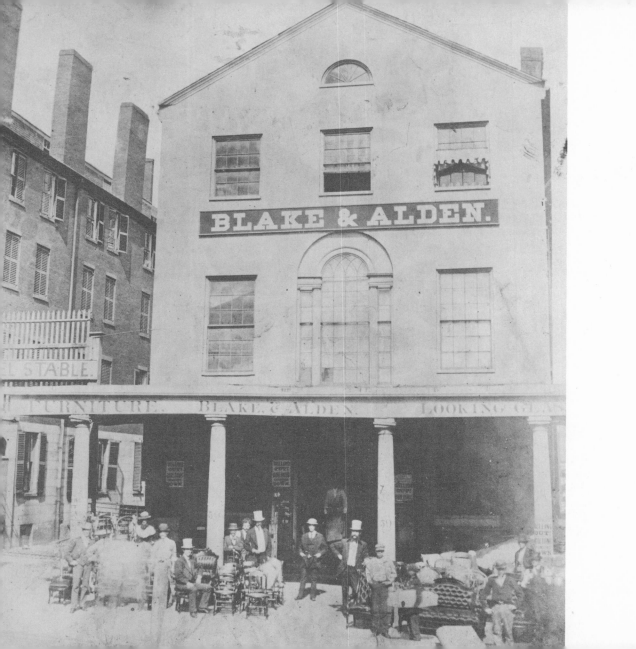

CORN OYSTERS

½ cup flour, sifted
¼ teaspoon baking powder
½ teaspoon salt
1 tablespoon milk
1 egg, well beaten
2 tablespoons butter or margarine, melted
1 cup cooked whole-kernel corn, drained
Cooking oil

Sift together the flour, baking powder and salt into mixing bowl. Combine the milk, egg and butter. Add the corn and mix well. Add and stir the corn mixture into the sifted dry ingredients; mix well. Pour oil about ¼-inch deep into a skillet. Heat the oil over medium heat. Drop the corn batter from a teaspoon into the hot oil. Brown the corn oyster quickly on both sides; drain on absorbent paper. Fritters should be the size of large oysters.
(Makes about 2 dozen)

NEW ENGLAND CORN PUDDING

3 eggs
3 tablespoons flour
¾ teaspoon salt
¼ teaspoon pepper
1 cup milk
1 cup heavy cream
3 tablespoons butter, melted
2 cups cooked whole-kernel corn

Preheat oven at 325°. Grease a 1½-quart casserole. Beat the eggs until light. Combine the flour, salt and pepper in a bowl; add to the eggs and beat until smooth. Slowly add and stir in the milk and cream. Stir in the butter. Add the corn and mix well. Turn the corn mixture into the prepared casserole; set the casserole in a pan and pour in hot water to within an inch of the top of the casserole. Bake 1 hour or until done.
(Makes 6-8 servings)

Blake And Alden, 59 Brattle Street

PUMPKIN WALNUT COOKIES

½ cup butter or margarine
1½ cups brown sugar
2 eggs
1 cup pumpkin
1 teaspoon vanilla
1 teaspoon lemon peel, grated
1 teaspoon lemon juice
2½ cups flour, sifted
3 teaspoons baking powder
1 teaspoon salt
1½ teaspoons pumpkin pie spice
¼ teaspoon ginger
1 cup walnuts, coarsely chopped
2 tablespoons sugar
½ teaspoon cinnamon

Cream butter and sugar together till fluffy. Beat in eggs, one at a time. Stir in pumpkin, vanilla, lemon peel and juice. Sift together flour, baking powder, salt, and spices. Blend into butter mixture. Stir in walnuts. Drop by rounded teaspoonfuls on greased cookie sheet one-inch apart. Sprinkle with sugar mixed with cinnamon. Bake at 375° 12 to 15 minutes.
(Makes about 4 dozen cookies)

PUMPKIN PIE

The colonists had learned to plant squash and pumpkins to counteract the effect of growing corn year after year on the soil As for the quantity available on the dinner table, one has only to read the following 17th century doggerel to figure it out:
We have pumpkins at morning
Pumpkins at noon.
If it were not for pumpkins
We should be undoon.

4 cups pumpkin, strained
4 eggs, beaten well
4 cups milk
1 cup molasses
2 teaspoons cinnamon
2 teaspoons ginger
2 teaspoons salt
Pastry for 1 9-inch pie

Boil the pumpkin in as little water as possible and drain, then strain through a sieve. Mix all together thoroughly and pour into pie plate lined with dough. Bake for 1 hour at 350°.

Boston Common laid out as a "trayning field" and a feeding place for "cattell". The cattle ceased to graze in 1830 but in the 1880's the training field still existed.

Hay Wagon On Boston Common

GREEN TOMATO PIE

6-8 medium green tomatoes, peeled
2 tablespoons lemon juice
1 teaspoon grated lemon or orange rind
½ teaspoon salt
¼ teaspoon cinnamon
½ cup sugar
2 tablespoons cornstarch
1 tablespoon butter or margarine
Pastry for 9-inch double crust pie

Combine tomatoes with lemon juice, rind, salt and cinnamon in saucepan and cook 15 minutes, stirring frequently. Mix sugar and cornstarch. Add to tomato mixture and cook until clear, stirring constantly. Add butter; cool slightly. Line pie plate with pastry and pour in mixture. Cover with pastry, seal edges and cut several gashes to allow steam to escape. Bake at 425° for 40-50 minutes. Serve slightly warm or cool.

BREAKFAST PIE

Pies have long been a Boston specialty. They are easy to eat and substantial fare whether eaten hot or cold. Breakfast was a particularly good time for pie. As Oliver Wendell Holmes tells us:
"— I will thank your for the pie, if you please. I took more of it than was good for me, — as much as 85°, I should think, — and had an indigestion in consequence. While I was suffering from it, I wrote some sadly desponding poems, and a theological essay which took a very melancholy view of creation. When I got better I labelled them all "Pie-Crust."
(The Autocrat at the Breakfast Table, by Oliver Wendell Holmes)

12 tablespoons shortening
1¾ cups flour, sifted
1 teaspoon salt
4 cups tart green apples, thinly sliced
⅔ cup sugar
½ teaspoon cinnamon
⅓ teaspoon nutmeg
2 tablespoons butter
⅔ cup, heavy cream

Cut shortening into flour and salt. When it looks like meal sprinkle cold water in until it holds together loosely. Roll out pastry and line a pie plate. Fill with sliced apples mixed with sugar. Sprinkle with cinnamon and nutmeg and bits of butter. Whip cream until thick and pour over apples. Put on top crust and seal the edges. Cover the top with a coating of egg white and sprinkle all lightly with sugar and bake at 375° until browned, about 40 minutes.

Horses And Wagons, Blackstone Street

CLAM CHOWDER

Several centuries ago, in the coastal villages of France, when a fishing fleet came home each man threw a share of his catch into a huge copper pot — la chaudière — and the community shared in a feast celebrating the safe return of the fishermen. The tradition found its way to Canada, then drifted down the coast to New England, where la chaudière became "chowder", any concoction made of fish or shellfish or both. The most famous of the American chowders is Clam Chowder.

1 quart clam with clam liquid
3 cups water
2 slices salt pork, chopped
1 medium onion, sliced
3 medium potatoes, diced
3 tablespoons butter
1¾ cups half-and-half (milk and cream)
1 tablespoon salt
¼ teaspoon white pepper

Combine clams, liquid, and water and cook to a boil Drain, reserving the broth. Mince the necks and the coarse membranes, chop the rest. Set all aside. Fry the salt pork until lightly browned; stir in onion, and cook until limp but not brown. Add the clam broth and potatoes and cook until potatoes are tender. Then stir in butter, half-and-half, salt, pepper, and clams. Heat, but do not boil. Pour immediately into warmed soup bowls. Serve with crackers.
(Makes 6-8 servings)

ESCALLOPED SCALLOPS

1½ pints scallops
1½ cups scallop liquid
1 pound mushrooms, sliced
1 green pepper, cut up
1 small onion, chopped
4 tablespoons butter
2 tablespoons flour
1 cup cream or milk
Salt and pepper to taste
¼ teaspoon paprika
Buttered bread Crumbs
½ cup white wine, optional

Parboil scallops for 5 minutes; reserve liquid. Drain, cool and cut up. Saute mushrooms, green pepper and onion in 2 tablespoons of butter until soft. Make cream sauce with remaining butter, flour, scallop liquid (½ cup wine may be substituted for ½ cup liquid), and milk or cream. Combine scallops, vegetables, and sauce in casserole, cover with crumbs, and bake at 400° for 10 minutes, or until brown.
(Makes 4 servings)

Pushcarts On Salem Street

PARSNIP STEW

There is nothing more heart-warming than this nourishing and economical dish. It conjures up the picture of the early settlers, kitchens, and the women who know how to best use the simple ingredients available. Parsnips were left in the ground throughout the winter, where they sweetened until the first spring thaw, and then were hustled into the kitchen pot.

2 slices salt pork
1 large onion, chopped fine
4 medium parsnips
4 large potatoes
¼ teaspoon salt
1 cup hot cream
Dumplings

Cut salt pork into small pieces. Fry until lightly browned. Add onion and cook until golden brown. Peel potatoes and add to parsnips. Combine with pork and onions. Add boiling water to cover. Add salt. Cook until vegetables are beginning to be tender, about 20 minutes. Add dumplings to top of stew. Cover and cook until light and tender, about 15 minutes. Remove dumplings to hot platter. Add cream to stew and pour over dumplings.

DUMPLINGS

1½ cups flour, sifted
2 teaspoons baking powder
¾ teaspoon salt
3 tablespoons butter or margarine
¾ cup milk

Sift together the flour, baking powder and salt. Add the butter and cut in with a pastry blender or 2 knives until mixture resembles coarse corn meal. Add milk and stir only until blended. Drop the dumpling dough on the stew by tablespoonfuls, making sure each dumpling rests on the vegetables.
(Makes 8-10 dumplings)

STRAWBERRY DUMPLINGS

1 quart strawberries
½ cup butter
¾ cup sugar
2 cups flour, sifted
3 teaspoons baking powder
½ teaspoon salt
¾ cup milk
Whipped cream, optional

Pick over and wash the strawberries. Mash until consistency of jam and add sugar to taste. Cream butter until very soft and mix thoroughly with the berry mixture. Place in refrigerator about 3 hours. About 20 minutes before serving, make the dumplings. Mix and sift flour, baking powder and salt. Add milk gradually, enough to make a soft dough. Drop dough from a tablespoon in little mounds close together in a buttered steamer. Place steamer over hot water and cover. Steam dumplings 10 to 15 minutes, until when broken with a fork, they are dry. Remove dumplings to a platter and pour strawberry mixture over them. Serve at once. Garnish each serving with whipped cream, if desired.
(Makes 4-6 servings)

Providence Depot In Park Square

POACHED SALMON WITH EGG SAUCE

From the earliest days it has been a tradition all through New England to serve Poached Salmon with Egg Sauce, with the season's new potatoes and early peas, on the Fourth of July. The eastern salmon began to "run" about this time, and the new vegetables were just coming in.

To poach salmon: Take a whole salmon or a 4 to 6-pound piece cut from center of the fish. Wrap the washed, cleaned salmon securely in a piece of cheesecloth, leaving long ends to expedite removing it from the broth when it is cooked. Bring to a boil 2 to 3 quarts of salted water (the amount depends on the amount of fish) containing 3 or 4 peppercorns, a bay leaf and a couple of slices of lemon. Boil for at least 15 minutes. Reduce heat until liquid is simmering add the salmon. Turn up the heat until it boils again, then reduce to simmer (it should be barely bubbling) until salmon is cooked. Figure on 6 to 8 minutes per pound. It is baked perfectly when it flakes easily. Take care not to overcook it. When the salmon is done, lift from the broth and remove the cheesecloth. Place on a hot serving platter and skin very carefully. Garnish with lemon and parsley. While salmon is cooking, make the egg sauce.

EGG SAUCE
1 cup milk
1 cup light cream
2 small onions, sliced
1 bay leaf
2 whole cloves
3 tablespoons butter
3 tablespoons flour
1 teaspoon salt
Dash white pepper
2 eggs, hard-boiled

Heat milk and cream together with the onion slices, bay leaf, and whole cloves until a film forms. Skim the surface. Melt butter in a saucepan; stir in flour, keeping it smooth, and cook over a very low heat for a few minutes. Pour in scalded milk mixture and cook over a low heat, stirring constantly, until mixture bubbles. Remove from heat; season with salt and pepper and strain into a saucepan. Add eggs, coarsely chopped, and heat through. If the sauce seems too thick, add a little more light cream. Serve separately in a warm sauceboat.

The first full cargo of bananas to reach the United States arrived at Long Wharf, Boston, in 1871. In March of that year, Captain L. Baker sailed the schooner, Telegraph, out of Provincetown for Port Antonio, Jamaica. There he took on his cargo of fruit and brought it back successfully to Boston.

At The Waterfront

OLD-FASHIONED SYLLABUB

To Make a Fine Syllabub from the Cow, Sweeten a quart of cyder with double refined sugar, grate nutmeg into it then milk your cow into your liquor, when you have thus added what quantity of milk you think proper, pour half a pint or more, in proportion to the quantity of syllabub you make, of the sweetest cream you can get all over it. (from American Cookery by Amelia Simmons, 1796)

American Cookery by Amelia Simmons was originally printed in 1796 in Hartford, Connecticut. It was the first American written cookbook to be published in the United States. And although not a Boston book, its influence was great on the early Boston cooks. The original volume contained 48 pages and sold well at 2 shillings, 3 pence a copy.

Washington Street

SYLLABUB

4 egg yolks
1 tablespoon flour
1 teaspoon vanilla
2 cups milk
¾ cup sugar
1 pint cream, whipped

Mix half the sugar with the flour. Bring milk to boiling point and add sugar and flour to it. Cook in a double boiler for 10 minutes. Beat the egg yolks, and add the other half of sugar to them. Now add this to the milk mixture, constantly stirring slowly. Cook 5 minutes; continue stirring. Remove from fire and add vanilla. Let mixture get cold. When serving fill a parfait glass half full of this custard and finish filling with whipped cream.
(Makes 4 servings)

OLD NEW ENGLAND SEED CAKE

1 cup sugar
2 tablespoons shortening
2 tablespoons butter
2 eggs
2½ cups milk
4 cups flour, sifted
¾ teaspoon salt
3 teaspoons baking powder
1 tablespoon caraway seeds
Candied orange peel, sliced

Preheat over to 350°. Grease 8-inch loaf pan. Sift flour, baking powder and salt together. Beat eggs. Cream sugar and shortening; add beaten eggs and beat very well. Add flour and milk alternately. Stir in caraway seeds and orange peel. Turn into prepared pan, and bake at 350° for 1 hour.

MRS. FRENCH'S POUND CAKE

Mrs. French's Pound Cake was used for suppers or sales at St. Anne's Church in Lowell, Massachusetts, in about 1840. It is especially nice cooked in little heart-shaped cakes.

1 cup butter
1 cup sugar
2 cups sifted flour
5 eggs
¼ teaspoon nutmeg
¼ teaspoon salt

Preheat oven to 325°. Butter an 8-inch loaf pan. Sift flour, salt and nutmeg. Cream butter and sugar until very soft and fluffy. Add beaten egg yolks and beat vigorously. Add flour a little at a time, beating well after each addition. When all the flour had been added, beat until mixture is smooth and velvety. Fold in well beaten egg whites. Turn into prepared pan and bake about 1 hour.

Causeway Street, 1884

CHINESE VEGETABLE SOUP

1 tomato
6 cups chicken stock
3 cups cabbage, shredded
½ cup carrot, sliced julienne-style
1 cup onion, thinly sliced
1 cup celery, sliced julienne-style
3 tablespoons oil
1 tablespoon salt
¼ teaspoon pepper
1 teaspoon sesame or salad oil
½ teaspoon Tabasco sauce

Blanch tomato in boiling water for a minute and slip off skin. Remove seeds and cut into small pieces. In boiling chicken stock, add cabbage, carrot, onion and celery, and bring to boil again. Reduce heat and cook until tender. Saute tomato in 3 tablespoons oil. Add to soup with salt and pepper. Cook for another 3 to 4 minutes, and add sesame oil or salad oil and Tabasco. Serve hot.
(Makes 4 servings)

FRIED CHICKEN PEKING STYLE

1 2-pound chicken
3 tablespoons Chinese cooking sherry
5 tablespoons soy sauce
5-inch leek, chopped
1 tablespoon ginger juice
Oil for frying

SAUCE

3 tablespoons soy sauce
1½ tablespoons vinegar
1 tablespoon sesame oil
½ tablespoon sugar
½ stalk leek, chopped
1 teaspoon ginger, minced
½ teaspoon garlic, minced

Soak chicken in mixture of wine, soy sauce, leek and ginger for about 1 hour. Heat oil and fry chicken in heavy skillet or wok. Drain and cut into small pieces about 2-inches long. Arrange these on plate. Mix sauce ingredients thoroughly, and pour sauce over chicken before serving.
(Makes 4 servings)

Buddhist Ceremony On Harrison Avenue, 1890

ARROWROOT PUDDING

Arrowroot is a nutritive, farinaceous substance manufactured from the roots of the several species of Maranta, a tropical American plant. The root was used by American Indians to absorb poison from arrow wounds.

1 quart milk
2 tablespoons arrowroot
¼ teaspoon salt
1½ tablespoons butter
¼ cup sugar
2 egg whites

Blend arrowroot, salt and sugar, with ¼ cup milk. Pour with remaining milk into top of double boiler. Add butter. Cook until mixture thickens, stirring all the time. Cool slightly; then fold in stiffly beaten egg whites. The pudding has a white creamy consistency. Chill and serve cold, topped with sauce.

SAUCE

2 egg yolks
½ cup sugar
1 cup milk
½ teaspoon vanilla

Beat yolks and sugar; add milk. Cook in top of small double boiler, stirring all the time until thick and smooth. Add vanilla. Makes a pure golden sauce. Cool and pour over each serving of pudding. (Makes 6 servings)

Marston's Dining Rooms, Brattle And Tremont Row

BUTTERSCOTCH PIE

1 cup brown sugar
¼ cup butter
¼ cup water
2 egg yolks
2 cups milk
1½ tablespoons flour
1 teaspoon vanilla
2 egg whites
½ cup sugar
One 9-inch baked pie shell

Boil brown sugar, butter and water until it waxes when a little is dropped from a spoon into cold water. Beat egg yolks; beat in flour, shaking a little at a time over yolks. Add milk and vanilla. Pour very slowly into brown sugar mixture, stirring all the time. Cook until thick, continuing to stir all of the time. Turn into baked pie shell. Let cool. Beat egg whites; add sugar, 2 tablespoons at a time. Pile lightly on top of pie filling and bake in oven at 325° until nicely browned, about 30 minutes.

BRAN BREAD

1½ cups flour
3 teaspoons baking powder
1 teaspoon salt
¼ cup sugar
1½ cups bran
½ cup dates, chopped
1 egg
¾ cup milk
½ cup maple syrup
4 tablespoons shortening, melted

Mix and sift the flour, baking powder, salt and sugar. Combine the bran and add dates, egg, milk, maple syrup and shortening. Mix thoroughly. Pour into 8 x 4-inch greased loaf pan. Bake at 350° for 50 minutes.

INDIAN PUDDING

The Indians are responsible for this dish. They used underground ovens made of stones, heated to necessary temperatures, in which food was allowed to remain until cooked. As time went on and improvements in cookery developed, doubtless this simple dish was modernized by the addition of flavoring to meet the popular taste.

2 cups milk
½ cup yellow corn meal
½ cup cold water
1 egg, slightly beaten
¼ cup sugar
½ cup molasses
1 teaspoon salt
1 teaspoon cinnamon
½ teaspoon ginger
2 cups milk
½ cup seedless raisins, optional
1 cup milk
Cream or vanilla ice cream

Scald the 2 cups milk in top of double boiler. Add corn meal, wet with cold water. Cook until thickened, stirring constantly. Cool to lukewarm. Add the egg, sugar, molasses, salt, cinnamon, ginger, 2 cups milk and raisins, if desired. Turn into well-buttered 2½ to 3-quart pudding dish. Bake at 300° for about 2 hours. Pour 1 cup milk over pudding and bake for 1 hour longer. Serve warm with cream or vanilla ice cream.
(Makes 4-6 servings)

At other periods, the Hancock Tavern was known as the Brazier Inn, kept by Madam Brazier, niece of Provincial Lieutenant Governor Phipps (1733). Here lodged Talleyrand in 1795, when exiled from France; also Louis Philippe, two years later and, in 1796, the exiled priest, John Cheverus, who later became the first Roman Catholic Bishop of Boston.

Old Hancock Tavern, Court Street, 1889

BOILED CAKE

1 cup raisins
1 cup sugar
1 cup water
½ cup shortening
1 teaspoon salt
1 teaspoon cinnamon
1 teaspoon nutmeg
½ teaspoon clove
½ teaspoon ginger
1 egg, beaten
1 teaspoon baking soda
2 cups flour, sifted

Preheat oven to 350°. Butter an 8-inch loaf pan. Combine raisins, sugar, water, shortening, salt and spices in a kettle and let boil five minutes. Remove from fire and cool slightly; then stir in the egg. Sift the flour and the baking soda, and add to the mixture. Pour into buttered loaf pan and bake 1 to 1¼ hours or until done.

APPLESAUCE CAKE

1 cup sugar
½ cup shortening
1 teaspoon salt
½ teaspoon cloves
¼ teaspoon nutmeg
1 cup raisins
1 teaspoon baking soda dissolved in a little warm water
1 cup applesauce
1¾ cups flour, sifted

Preheat oven to 350°. Butter an 8-inch loaf pan. Cream sugar and shortening. Add salt, cloves, nutmeg and raisins. Add baking soda that has been dissolved in warm water and stir in the applesauce. Beat until well mixed. Add flour and combine. Bake in preheated oven for 45 minutes.

Interior Of 130 Mill Street

JOHNNY CAKES

Maize or Indian corn was given to America by the Indians. Its origin has long been in dispute. But we can assume the primitive corncob dates from about 3000 B.C. It is generally accepted that it originated in the jungles of Guatemala and the Yucatan and was the main foodstuff of the Maya Indians. Knowledge of it passed to the Incas, the Aztecs and finally to the North American Indians. During the many years of cultivation, it developed from a kind of coarse grass with a tiny ear to the plant we know today. Aside from wild game and fish, corn became the principal item of food in the New World. Even Columbus is credited with writing of its nutritional value as well as the Indian use of corn in his report to Queen Isabella in 1492. When the Pilgrims landed at Plymouth in 1620, the winter was bleak with most of the wheat brought from England spoiled from the long ship voyage. But luck led Miles Standish to the discover of a cache of corn stored by the Indians. The kindness of Squanto, a Putexet Indian, taught the settlers how to pound corn into meal with a crude mortar and pestle. Then they learned how to mix it with water to form a stiff dough. When flattened and before an open fire, it became a sort of cake, the original Johnnycake, taking its name from the fact that these little cakes travelled well. They first were called journeycakes and later became johnnycakes, the name we know today.

1 cup white corn meal
¾ teaspoon salt
1 cup water
½ cup milk
Bacon drippings

Put the corn meal and salt into a medium-size mixing bowl. Bring the water to a rapid boil. With the pan in one hand, let the boiling water dribble onto the corn meal while stirring constantly with the other. Then stir the milk into the mixture; it will be fairly thick, not runny. Heat a griddle or heavy skillet and grease it generously with the bacon drippings. Drop the batter, by spoonfuls, onto the griddle. Flatten them with a spatula or fork to a thickness of about ¼-inch. Fry until brown, then turn and brown on the other side, adding more drippings as necessary. Serve hot with butter, maple syrup or applesauce. They are also good with bacon and eggs or topped with creamed chipped beef. (Makes 4 servings)

Panoramic View Of The North End

BAKED SWEET POTATOES AND APPLES

3 large tart apples
3 large cooked sweet potatoes
Butter or margarine
¾ teaspoon salt
⅓ cup maple syrup

Pare and core the apples. Cut into ½-inch thick crosswise slices. Peel and cut sweet potatoes into thick slices; set potatoes aside. Set oven for 350°. Butter a shallow baking dish. Melt about 2 tablespoons of the butter in a skillet over medium heat. Put the apple slices into the skillet and sauté until golden brown and almost tender; turn once. Place the sweet potato slices in the prepared baking dish. Sprinkle with the salt. Arrange the apple slices on the sweet potato slices. Pour the maple syrup over all and dot with butter. Bake 40 minutes or until thoroughly heated and brown.
(Makes 6 servings)

SCALLOPED POTATOES

6 cups potatoes, pared and thinly sliced
2 cups onions, thinly sliced
5 tablespoons flour
4 tablespoons butter
2 cups hot milk
Salt and pepper
Paprika

Preheat oven to 400°. Arrange layer of potatoes in buttered casserole. Cover with layer of onions. Sprinkle with some flour, salt and pepper; dot with some butter. Repeat layers until all ingredients are used, ending with butter. Pour hot milk over all ingredients and sprinkle with paprika. Lower oven to 350° and bake one hour or until tender.
(Makes 4 servings)

Considered the oldest brick building still standing in Boston, the Ebenezer Hancock House was first occupied in 1660 by William Courser, first town crier of Boston and in 1737 by James Davenport, brother-in-law of Benjamin Franklin. Ebenezer was the brother of John Hancock and deputy paymaster of the Continental Army during the Revolution. Here were stored the French crowns sent by the King of France to finance the war.

Ebenezer Hancock House On Marshall Street

BAKED BEANS

Beans have a long tradition in Boston. Originally, they were baked in the family's bean hole, a small hole in the ground lined with stone. Here a fire was built in the hole to heat the stone; then a covered pot of beans would be placed in the hold and sealed with stones or branches. It was a very popular dish on the Sabbath because no work was supposed to be done. So often on Saturday morning or Friday night the beans were started. The first big pot was eaten with brown bread on Saturday night. Although it was still the Sabbath, serving was not forbidden. The remains were left in the oven where they kept warm for Sunday breakfast or possibly for their return from Church in the afternoon. The Puritan Sabbath died out in the 19th century but Baked Beans and Brown Bread kept their popularity as Saturday night fare.

6 cups pea or navy beans
1 pound salt pork
1 tablespoon dry mustard
1 tablespoon salt
1 teaspoon black pepper
1 cup molasses
1 small onion, optional

Pick over beans, cover with cold water, and soak overnight. In the morning, drain, cover with fresh water, bring to a boil very slowly, then simmer until the skins burst. Drain beans. Scald the salt pork, which should be well streaked with lean, by letting it stand in boiling water for 5 to 10 minutes. Cut off two thin slices, one to place in bottom of pot, the other to be cut into bits. Score rind of the remaining piece with a sharp knife. Mix dry mustard, salt, black pepper, and molasses. Alternate the layers of beans in the pot with the molasses mixture and the bits of pork. If you use an onion, bury it in the middle. When the bean pot is full, push the large piece of pork down into the beans with the rind sticking up. Add boiling water to cover, put the lid on, and bake all day (a minimum of 6 to 8 hours) in a 250° oven. Check from time to time and add boiling water if needed. Uncover pot during last hour of baking so the rind can brown and crisp.
(Makes 10-12 servings)

Washington Street From Winter Street

73

BAKED HAM

10 to 12 pound ready-to-eat ham
Whole cloves
¾ cup fine dry bread crumbs
¾ cup maple sugar
1 egg, beaten
Apple cider

Preheat oven to 325°. Place ham, fat side up, on a rack in a shallow baking pan. Bake ham allowing 15 minutes per pound. About 45 minutes before the end of the baking period, remove ham from oven. Slit ham rind with scissors and peel off. Using a sharp knife, make cuts ¼-inch deep in the ham fat in a diamond pattern. Stud fat with the whole cloves. Combine the bread crumbs with the sugar. Brush the ham with the beaten egg. Pat the bread crumb-sugar mixture over the ham. Slowly spoon the apple cider over the bread crumb-sugar mixture. Return the ham to the oven and bake remaining 45 minutes or until brown; baste often with cider.
(Makes 10-12 servings)

BOSTON BROWN BREAD

"It was a common saying among the Puritans," Matthew Henry reported in his Commentaries, published in the early eighteenth century, "'Brown bread and the Gospel is good fare.'"

1 cup rye flour
1 cup corn meal
1 cup Graham flour
¾ teaspoon baking soda
1 teaspoon salt
¾ cup molasses
2 cups buttermilk
1 cup chopped raisins, optional

Sift all dry ingredients together; add molasses, buttermilk, raisins. Divide batter and place in 2 buttered 1-quart pudding molds or 3 buttered 1-pound coffee cans, filling them about ¾ full. Molds must be covered tightly, with buttered lids tied and taped so the bread won't force the cover off on rising. Place molds in a pan filled with enough boiling water to reach halfway up the mold and steam for 3 hours, keeping water at the halfway mark. Serve piping hot with butter and Boston Baked Beans.

According to the census of 1880, the number of establishments engaged in manufacturing and mechanical industries was 3,520. The number of hands employed was 56,813; of whom 37,831 were males over 16; of whom 17,753 were females over 15 and of whom 1,229 were children.

Workshop Of Macullar Parker Co., Clothing Manufacturers, Est. 1849

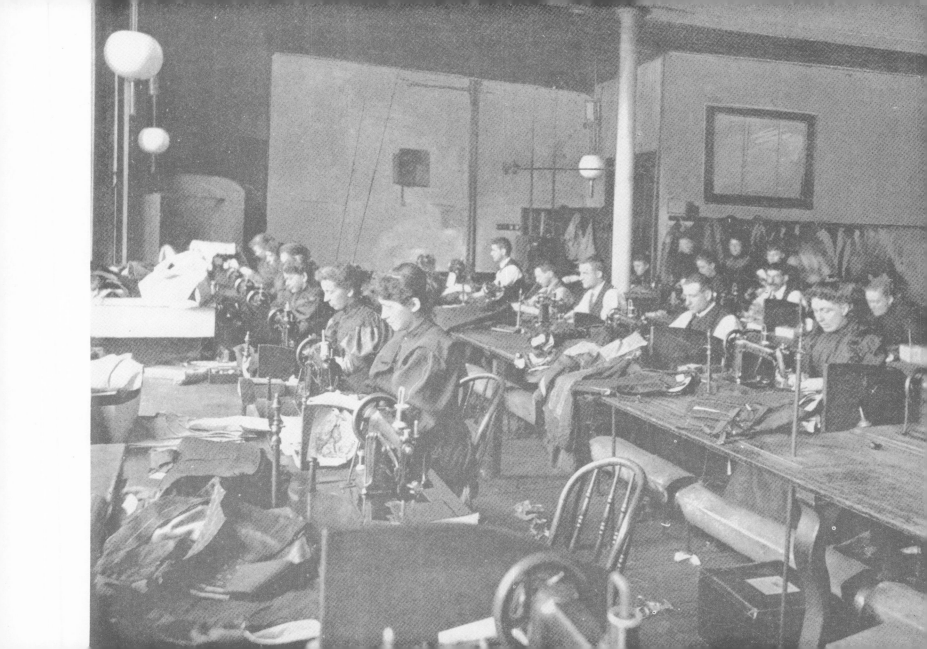

SNOW PUDDING

5 egg whites
3 lemons
1 tablespoon unflavored gelatin
¼ cup cold water
½ cup sugar

Heat lemon juice; add gelatin after softening in cold water. Stir until smooth. Cool and fold in stiffly beaten egg whites. Chill. Serve in parfait glasses with yankee sauce.
(Makes 6-8 servings)
(*Adapted from an old recipe*)

YANKEE SAUCE
1 cup butter
2 cups confectioners' sugar
2 tablespoons cornstarch
¼ cup cold water
1 pint boiling water
2 teaspoons cider vinegar
1 teaspoon vanilla

Cream butter and sugar together until smooth. Combine cornstarch with cold water, and add to boiling water. Cook until clear and no starch taste remains, about 15 minutes. Add butter and sugar mixture, vinegar and vanilla. Serve warm.
(Makes 3 cups)

SNOW BALL COOKIES

½ cup butter
1 egg
1 cup sugar
1 cup dates, chopped
2 cups rice cereal
½ cup pecans, chopped
½ teaspoon vanilla
Coconut

Mix the butter, egg, sugar and dates. Cook in double boiler for 20 minutes. Take off heat. Add the rice cereal, pecans and vanilla. Spoon into small balls and roll in coconut. Chill in refrigerator.
(Makes about 25 cookies)

Head Of Park Street In Winter

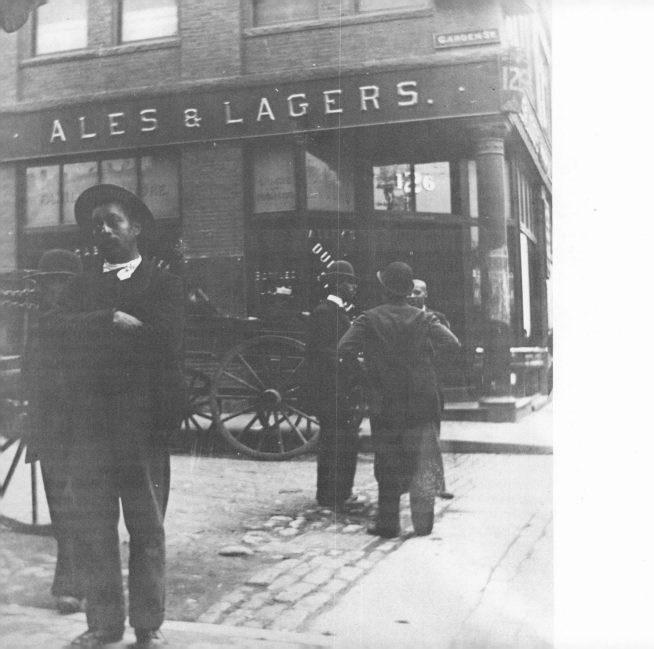

GINGER BEER

4 cups sugar
Juice of 4 lemons
24 cups cold water
2 teaspoons ginger, ground
1 teaspoon tartaric acid
Sultana raisins

Combine sugar, lemon juice, cold water, ground ginger and tartaric acid in a very large bowl. Stir until sugar dissolves. Strain into hot sterilized bottles. Add 3 Sultana raisins to each bottle. Cork bottle. When the raisins rise to the top in 3 to 4 days, the ginger beer is ready.

ROOT BEER

Take one and one-half gallons of molasses, add five gallons of water at 60°. Let this stand two hours; then pour into a barrel, and add one-quarter pound powdered or bruised sassafras bark, one-quarter pound powdered or bruised wintergreen bark, one-quarter pound bruised sarsaparilla root, one-half pint yeast, water enough to fill the small barrel. Ferment for twelve hours and bottle
(From old-Time Recipes for Home Made Wines and Liqueurs compiled by Helen S. Wright, Boston, 1909)

Here in the West End, America's most noted architect Charles Bulfinch, was born; also here, but now vanished was the long famous Revere House where the royalty of many lands, a president of the United States and many other famous personages enjoyed the hospitality and the celebrated cuisine of this historic hotel.

In The West End

OLD-FASHIONED DOUGHNUTS

4½ cups flour, sifted
4 teaspoons baking powder
½ teaspoon salt
¼ teaspoon nutmeg
¼ cup shortening
1 cup sugar
2 eggs
1 cup milk
Fat or cooking oil
Sugar

Sift the flour, baking powder, salt and nutmeg together. Put the shortening in a large mixing bowl and beat until fluffy. Gradually add and beat in the sugar. Add the eggs, one at a time, beating well after each addition. Add the dry ingredients, a little at a time, alternately with the milk, stirring after each addition to blend well. Cover the bowl and chill the dough about 1 hour. Roll out the dough to a thickness of about ¼-inch. Cut with a doughnut cutter. Fry in fat or cooking oil. Drain the doughnuts on absorbent paper. Sprinkle with sugar, if desired.
(Makes about 2 dozen)

EMILY'S BLACK CAKE

As Emily Dickinson in the Broadway play, "The Belle of Amherst", Julie Harris opens the play by sharing with the audience the "receipt" for Miss Dickinson's Black Cake. Emily Dickinson lived all her life in Amherst, Massachusetts and was long encouraged in her writing by Thomas W. Higginson, Cambridge writer, who published the first two volumes of Miss Dickinson's poems in 1890.

½ pound sugar
½ pound butter
5 eggs
¼ pint molasses
½ pound flour, sifted
½ teaspoon baking soda
1 teaspoon each: cloves, mace cinnamon
½ teaspoon nutmeg, ground
¼ pint brandy
1 pound raisins
⅔ pound currants
⅔ pound citron, diced

Add sugar to softened butter, blending until light and creamy. Add eggs and molasses and beat this mixture well. Resift flour together with the baking soda, cloves, mace, cinnamon and nutmeg. Gradually add sifted ingredients to the butter-egg-sugar mixture, alternating with the brandy and beating thoroughly. Then stir in the raisins, currants, and citron. Pour the dough into two loaf pans lined with a layer of heavy waxed paper and bake for 3 to 4 hours at 300°. (Place a shallow pan of hot water in the bottom of the oven, but remove it for the last half hour of baking.) Loaves will be done when a straw inserted in center comes out clean and surfaces spring back to the touch. Cool. Store in tins in cool place.

The first newspapers of the New World were published in Boston. The very first venture was attempted in 1690 with the publication of "Public Occurrences Both Forreign and Domestick" printed by Richard Pierce for Benjamin Harris at the "London Coffee House". It came to an end after a single issue.

Newspaper Row

CRANBERRY PIE

The Indians had learned to pound the wild cranberries from the sand dunes with dried meat in a mortar. Thus, combined with melted animal fat, they concocted pemmican, which helped keep them through the long hard winter. Consequently, it is not surprising that the first Thanksgiving dinner in 1621 included cranberries. They had been served tart since sugar was unheard of until later when trade was established with the West Indies and sugar and molasses exchanged for salt fish. Only then did people have cranberry sauce as we know it. Cranberries were early recognized as a good preventive of scurvy, and ships putting out to sea from Down East ports always carried casks of this "bogland medicine" in their stores. Though they are now commercially grown in Wisconsin, Washington, Oregon, and New Jersey, cranberries were associated first with Massachusetts.

2 cups fresh cranberries
1½ cups sugar, divided
½ cup nuts, chopped
2 eggs
1 cup flour
½ cup butter, melted
¼ cup shortening, melted

Grease a 10-inch pie plate well. Spread cranberries over bottom; sprinkle with ½ cup sugar and nuts. Beat eggs well. Add 1 cup sugar gradually; beat until well mixed. Add flour, melted butter and shortening to egg-sugar mixture. Beat well. Pour batter over cranberries and bake at 325° for 60 minutes, until crust is golden brown. Cut like pie. Serve warm or cold with vanilla ice cream.

CRANBERRY MUFFINS

¾ cup cranberries, coarsely chopped
½ cup confectioners' sugar
2 cups flour, sifted
3 teaspoons baking powder
½ teaspoon salt
1 teaspoon cinnamon
¼ teaspoon nutmeg
¼ cup sugar
1 egg, well beaten
1 cup milk
¼ cup shortening, melted

Preheat oven to 350°. Grease muffin pans well. Mix together the cranberries and confectioners' sugar, and let stand while preparing the batter. Sift the flour, baking powder, salt, cinnamon, nutmeg and sugar into a mixing bowl. Combine the egg, milk and shortening and add, all at once, to the dry ingredients. Stir just until the dry ingredients are dampened. Do not beat. Fold in the cranberries. Fill the muffin tins ⅔ full. Bake in preheated oven for 20 minutes or until brown. (Makes 12-14 muffins)

The Old Corner Bookstore lingers as a weathered relic of the past in one of Boston's busiest business districts. It dates from 1712 and became a book stand in 1828 although booksellers left it in 1903. Its interest lies in its literary associations during the golden age of Boston literary activity.

Old Corner Bookstore, Washington And School Streets

POTATO ROLLS

1½ cups hot riced potato
½ cup butter
8 cups flour
1 cake compressed yeast
3 tablespoons sugar
2 cups milk
1 cup water
1 tablespoon salt

Scald milk; add potato, butter, sugar and salt; beat briskly and cool to lukewarm. Dissolve yeast in warm water and add potato mixture. Stir in flour and knead thoroughly. Cover, let rise in a warm place until dough doubles in bulk, about two hours. Punch down; knead lightly and shape in rolls. Place in well-greased baking pans; let rise and brush with melted butter. Bake at 375° 20 minutes, or until done.
(Makes 48 rolls)
(*Adapted from an old recipe*)

POTATO SOUP

1 large carrot
1 large onion
2 large potatoes
1 tablespoon butter
1 quart milk
1 tablespoon parsley, chopped
Salt and pepper

Boil carrots, onions and potatoes. Press through a colander; add salt and pepper to taste. Add butter and milk; heat to boiling. Garnish with chopped parsley.
(Makes 4 servings)

Corner Of Court Street And Cornhill

BOILED CIDER PIE

1 cup sugar
¼ cup water
2 tablespoons butter
2 pastry crusts for 8-inch pie
17 tablespoons boiled cider
2 eggs, separated
Nutmeg, grated

Combine sugar, water, butter and thick boiled cider; simmer about 15 minutes. Cool. Add egg yolks, well beaten. Fold in egg white that have been beaten stiff. Line an 8-inch pie plate with the unbaked pie crust. Pour in filling. Sprinkle with nutmeg. Add the top crust and bake at 450° for 10 minutes; then reduce heat to 350° for 30 minutes. For best results, use sweet cider boiled until it is thick and dark. The pie will run a little. It does not completely set.

DOWN EAST CRABS

2 cups crab meat
¼ cup dry sherry
2 egg yolks, well beaten
3 tablespoons flour
1 teaspoon salt
1 teaspoon dry mustard
Dash pepper
3 tablespoons butter or margarine
2 cups milk
Few drops Tabasco sauce
Buttered bread crumbs

Preheat oven to 375°. Grease crab shells or a 1-quart baking dish. Put the crab meat in a bowl. Pour the wine and egg yolks over the crab; toss to mix well. Put the flour, salt, mustard and pepper in a small dish; stir until blended. Melt the butter in a saucepan over low heat; add and blend in the flour mixture. Stir in milk and Tabasco sauce. Cook over low heat, stirring constantly, until the mixture comes to a boil. Cook and stir 3 to 5 minutes longer until thickened. Slowly pour and stir the hot sauce over the crab mixture; mix well. Divide among the crab shells or turn into the casserole. Sprinkle the crumbs on top. Bake in preheated oven 10 to 15 minutes or until brown.
(Makes 6 servings)

"The Hackney-carriage and cab system of the city, though occasionally complained of by fastidious citizens, is a great improvement over that suffered in Boston for many years . . . Every hackney carriage is licensed and has permission to stand at a specified place. The fare for an adult for short distances, from one place to another in the city proper is 50 cents."
(*Edwin Bacon, 1883*)

Hackney Carriage In Front Of Hotel Thorndike, Boylston Street

PANNED OYSTERS

¼ cup butter or margarine
1 pint oysters, drained
1½ tablespoons lemon juice
Worcestershire sauce
Hot toast
Lemon wedges

Melt the butter over low heat in a heavy skillet. Add the oyster and cook over low heat just until edges of oysters curl. Stir in lemon juice. Season oysters with salt and pepper and a dash of Worcestershire sauce. Serve the panned oyster on the hot toast. Spoon pan juices over all; garnish with lemon wedges.
(Makes 3-4 servings)

SCALLOPED OYSTERS

¾ cup cracker crumbs
¾ cup fine dry bread crumbs
½ cup butter or margarine, melted
1 pint small oysters, drained
Salt and pepper
1½ cups milk
½ cup heavy cream
¼ cup oyster liquid

Set oven for moderately hot, 375°. Grease a 1½-quart casserole. Combine the cracker crumbs and the bread crumbs. Add the melted butter and mix well. Cover the bottom of the casserole with a think layer of buttered crumbs. Put a layer of the oysters over the crumbs in the casserole. Sprinkle with salt and pepper. Combine the milk, cream and oyster liquid; mix well. Pour half of the milk mixture over the oysters. Sprinkle a layer of crumbs over the oysters. Place remaining oysters on crumbs and sprinkle with salt and pepper. Pour remaining milk mixture over oysters and cover with the remaining crumbs. Bake 25 to 30 minutes or until heated.
(Makes 4 servings)

Tremont Street Mall

CHICKEN BROTH

One 3-4 pound fowl
½ pound salt pork
3 potatoes
2 onions
1½ tablespoons flour
5 tablespoons cornmeal
1 teaspoon onion, minced
½ teaspoon sage
2 teaspoons salt

Cover the fowl with cold water; bring to a boil. Add salt; reduce heat and simmer until nearly tender. Add sliced potatoes and onions, and cook until tender. Lift out fowl and use for salad or creamed chicken. Strain broth; add sage, minced onion and the flour and cornmeal after mixing them with cold water. Boil until slightly thickened. Veal may be cooked in the same way.
(Makes 6-8 servings)
(*Adapted from an old recipe*)

YEAST RUSKS

1 cup milk
1 cup butter
½ cup sugar
¼ cup water
1 teaspoon salt
1 teaspoon nutmeg
1 teaspoon baking soda
2 eggs
1 cake compressed yeast

Scald milk; cool to lukewarm. Add well-beaten eggs, yeast dissolved in water and enough flour to make a moderately stiff dough. Cover; put in warm place and let rise until light, about two hours. Knead in softened butter, sugar, baking soda and nutmeg. Cover; let rise in a warm place until dough doubles in bulk; punch down, knead. Roll out and cut or mold into flat rounds. Place in a well-greased baking pan and when rusks have risen until light, bake at 400° for 20 minutes. Brush the top with lightly beaten egg white. Sprinkle with sugar and return to the oven for one minute. Serve hot.
(Makes about 2 dozen rusks)

In 1862 the present iron fence was built around the Public Garden, the enclosure graded, filled and definitely laid out as a garden. The first swanboats in America appeared on Boston's Public Garden in 1877. The year before, Robert Piaget capitalized on the popularity of the bicycle-built-for-two with two-seater paddle skiffs (with a seat for the driver). However, traffic was so heavy he developed the larger craft.

Swan Boats In Boston Public Garden

91

OLD-FASHIONED PORK CAKE

1 pound salt pork
2 cups boiling water
1 pound raisins
1 pound currants
2 cups nuts
1 teaspoon cloves
7 cups flour
½ teaspoon baking soda
6 teaspoons baking powder
2 teaspoons cinnamon
2 cups brown sugar
1 cup molasses
4 tablespoons strong coffee
1 tablespoon vanilla
½ cup citron

Sift flour with baking soda and baking powder; chop pork very fine. Add boiling water; mix well and stand until cool. Mix other ingredients and add to pork mixture; mix well. Put into 3 greased 8-inch loaf pans. Bake at 350° about 2½ hours.
(Makes 3 loaves)

BEAN POT APPLESAUCE

8 medium tart apples
⅔ cup brown sugar
½ teaspoon cinnamon
Apple cider

Pare, quarter and core the apples. Combine sugar and cinnamon. Put a layer of apples in bottom of the bean pot; sprinkle some of the sugar mixture over them, and continue layering until all ingredients are used. Pour apple cider over the apples to cover completely. Cover bean pot; place in oven at 350° and bake 2 to 3 hours, or until apples are tender.
(Makes 4-6 servings)

Court Street, Ames Building And Young's Hotel

APPLE CHUTNEY

4 pounds onion, chopped
4½ cups brown sugar
1 pound raisins
2 teaspoons cloves, ground
1 tablespoon salt
3 pounds apples, pared and chopped
3 tablespoons molasses
2 teaspoons ginger
1 tablespoon cinnamon
Dash cayenne

Combine all ingredients in large kettle; simmer uncovered, stirring occasionally for 2 hours, or until mixture becomes thick and dark. Pour into hot sterilized jars; seal at once. Excellent with lamb, pork, or ham. (Makes 6 pints)

BOSTON HOT

1 peck ripe tomatoes
2 cups celery
3 sweet red peppers
3 sweet green peppers
2 cups sweet onions
1 cup horseradish root
1 cup white mustard seed
1 cup brown sugar
⅔ cup salt
6 cups sugar
2 tablespoons mixed pickling spice

Chop all vegetables fairly fine; drain tomatoes and combine all ingredients. Heat to boiling point but do not cook. Seal in sterilized jars. (Makes 5 quarts)

The "Great House" of the governor, in which the Court of Assistants adopted the order giving Boston its name in 1630, stood on the west side of City Square. The home of the young minister, John Harvard, stood nearby. The date of its foundation as a town, as stated by Richard Frothingham, Charlestown's historian, was 1629 though an earlier date has been claimed. It flourished in the colonial period, and on account of the battle of Bunker Hill in 1775, and its burning by the British at that time, it became conspicuous at the beginning of the Revolution. In the late 1800's, Charlestown, then annexed to Boston, was considered an old-fashioned, quaint place.

City Square, Charlestown

PARSNIP FRITTERS

4 to 6 medium parsnips
Boiling salted water
1 egg, slightly beaten
2 tablespoons butter, melted
Flour
Salt and pepper
Cooking oil

Scrub the parsnips; place in a saucepan. Cover with boiling salted water and cook over medium heat 30 minutes or until parsnips are tender. Drain the parsnips and peel off the skins. Put the parsnips in a bowl and mash them. Add the egg, butter, about 2 tablespoons of flour, and salt and pepper to taste. Shape the parsnip mixture into 6 patties and dip them in flour. Pour cooking oil about ¼-inch in a skillet. Fry the parsnip fritters until golden brown, turning to brown evenly.
(Makes 6 servings)

MUSTARD PICKLES

1 quart small white onions
1 medium cauliflower
1 quart gherkins
Salt
Water
2½ cups sugar
6 tablespoons dry mustard
1½ tablespoons turmeric
2 tablespoons celery seed
1 quart vinegar
1 sweet red pepper, seeded and chopped
¼ cup flour

Peel the onions. Remove the leaves and core of the cauliflower and discard. Break the cauliflower into flowerets. Leave small gherkins whole. Cut large ones into 3 or 4 pieces. Wash the vegetables in cold water and drain. Place the vegetables in an earthenware crock or large bowl. Add the drained vegetables and the pepper to the vinegar mixture. Bring the mixture to a boil, stirring frequently; reduce heat and simmer 15 minutes. Combine flour with a little water to make a smooth paste. Add some of the hot vinegar mixture to the flour; slowly stir flour mixture into the kettle. Cook and stir until mixture comes to a boil and thickens. Spoon the hot mixture into hot sterilized jars and seal at once.
(Makes about 6 pints)

The Hurdy Gurdy

JACOB WIRTH'S SAUERBRATEN

4 pound beef for pot roast
2 teaspoons salt
1 teaspoon ginger, ground
2 cups cider vinegar
2½ cups water
2 medium onions, sliced
3 tablespoons mixed pickling spice
3 bay leaves
1 teaspoon peppercorns
8 whole cloves
⅓ cup sugar
2 tablespoons fat
Flour or gingersnaps

Rub meat with salt and ginger; put in large bowl. Combine remaining ingredients except fat and flour; bring to boil and pour over meat. Cool. Cover and put in refrigerator for 3 days. Turn meat once each day. Remove meat from pickling liquid and reserve liquid. Dry meat with paper towel. Brown meat on all sides in fat in heavy kettle. Put on rack; add 1 cup reserved pickling liquid and half the onions and spices from liquid. Cover and simmer for 3½ hours or until tender, adding more liquid if needed. Remove meat to hot platter. Strain liquid in pan and return to heat; strain in additional pickling liquid to make about 2 cups. Skim off excess fat. Thicken gravy with a little flour mixed with cold water or thicken with 6 crumbled gingersnaps.
(Makes 6 servings)

Beer Haulers In Front Of Jacob Wirth's Restaurant, circa 1890

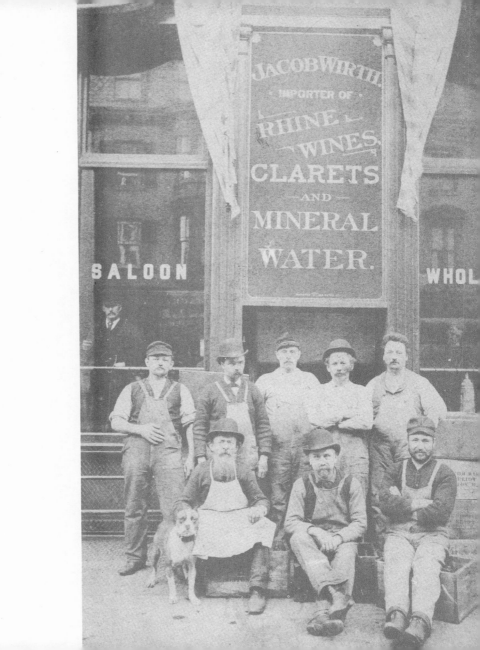

SUMMER SQUASH PICKLES

4 medium summer squash (about 2 pounds)
½ cup coarse salt
½ cup sugar
1½ cups white vinegar
3 tablespoons dry mustard
1 tablespoon ginger, ground
1 tablespoon curry powder
6 peppercorns

Peel squash; halve, seed and cut into ½-inch cubes. Layer with salt in a large bowl. Cover bowl with a towel. Let stand overnight. Then drain and rinse squash in cold water and place in heavy kettle. Combine sugar, vinegar and spices in a heavy saucepan. Heat to boiling. Boil for 5 minutes and pour over squash. Cook about 5 minutes or until squash is tender. Pour into hot, sterilized jars and seal.
(Makes 2 pounds)

PUMPKIN CHIPS

One 3-pound pumpkin
6 cups sugar
Juice and grated rind of 3 lemons
Dash salt

Pare pumpkins; remove seed and stringy portion. Cut into ½-inch squares about ¼-inch thick. Combine with sugar, grated lemon rind and salt. Let stand overnight. Cook slowly until pumpkin becomes transparent and syrup thickens, stirring to prevent sticking. Add lemon juice; cook for 15 minutes longer. Pour into hot, sterilized jars and seal. Serve as a relish for meat.
(Makes about 3 pints)

Entrance To The Park Street Subway

MOCK CHERRY PIE

2 cups cranberries, coarsely chopped
1 cup raisins, coarsely chopped
1¼ cups sugar
1½ tablespoons flour
¼ teaspoon salt
½ teaspoon vanilla
¼ cup boiling water
Pastry for 2 crust 9-inch pie
Cream

Make the pastry for a two-crust pie. Use lattice strips on top. For filling, mix cranberries, raisins, sugar, flour, salt and vanilla. Stir to remove lumps. Add water. Cook 10 minutes. Cool. Put in pastry lined pie plate. Brush lattice strips with cream and press edges firmly together. Bake at 425° for about 30 minutes.
(Makes 6 servings)

GOLDEN CORN BREAD

¼ cup shortening
3 tablespoons sugar
1 egg
¾ cup yellow cornmeal
½ cup flour, sifted
1½ teaspoons baking powder
1½ teaspoons salt
1 cup cooked squash
½ cup milk

Cream shortening and sugar. Add egg and beat. Combine cornmeal, flour, baking powder and salt. Add milk to squash. Add dry ingredients to egg mixture, alternately with liquid. Pour into greased 8-inch square pan. Bake at 350° for 20 to 25 minutes.
(Makes 6 servings)

The bookstores of Boston had for many years been favorite gathering places for literary and professional men. For a long time the "Old Corner Bookstore" was the principal authors' meeting place where one could readily see Longfellow, Lowell, Hawthorne, Holmes, Whittier, Emerson and others.

Old Corner Bookstore Block, Washington Street

BAKED COD

Cod was once the main source of food for all New England. The fishing industry, as early as 1640, depended greatly on the cod supply. So important was the "sacred cod" that a wooden replica has been hanging on display at the Boston State House since 1784.

4 pounds fresh cod
2-inch cube of salt pork
1 onion, sliced
6 cups potatoes, thinly sliced
4 cups milk
1 tablespoon salt
¼ teaspoon pepper
3 tablespoons butter
8 common crackers, split in half

Clean and skin the fish. Be sure to keep the head, tail, backbone, and other trimmings. Cut the cod into 2-inch pieces and set aside. Put head, tail, and all the trimmings in a saucepan with 2 cups of water. Heat to the boiling point, then reduce heat, and cook slowly about 20 minutes. Cut salt pork into small pieces and fry over a low heat until crisp. Stir in onion slices and cook until limp. Parboil potato slices for 5 minutes (use enough boing water to cover). Drain. Add the potatoes and 2 cups of boiling water to salt-pork mixture. Cook 5 minutes. Add liquid drained from fish bones, then add the cod. Cover and simmer for 10 minutes. Scald milk; pour into fish mixture. Add salt, pepper, butter and crackers. Heat until very hot.
(Makes 6-8 servings)

Boston Common, Showing State House

CODFISH CAKES

2 cups flaked salt codfish
4 medium potatoes
2 eggs
2 tablespoons butter or margarine
Dash pepper
Fat or cooking oil

Freshen the fish according to package directions or soak it in water overnight. Drain well. Pare the potatoes and cut in quarters. Put the potatoes and fish in a saucepan with water to cover. Cook until tender and drain well. Beat until the potatoes are mashed. Beat the eggs; stir the eggs, butter and pepper into the potato mixture. Shape into flat cakes. Pour fat to a depth of about ¼-inch into a skillet. Fry the cakes until brown, turning once. Serve with baked beans and brown bread. (Makes 6 servings)

SOUR CREAM BISCUITS

1 cup flour, sifted
1½ teaspoons baking powder
¼ teaspoon baking soda
1 tablespoon sugar
½ teaspoon salt
¼ cup shortening
½ cup sour cream
Cream, optional

Sift flour, baking powder, baking soda, sugar and salt. Work in shortening with blender. Add sour cream. Mix only until blended. Turn out onto lightly-floured board and knead lightly for about 30 seconds. Pat to ½-inch thickness. Cut with floured 2-inch biscuit cutter. Bake on ungreased baking sheet at 450° for about 15 minutes. Tops of biscuits may be brushed with cream before baking to give browner crust. (Makes 6 biscuits for shortcake)

SEA FOOD NEWBURG

2 cups cooked lobster, crabmeat, shrimps and scallops
½ cup butter
¼ cup sherry
2 tablespoons brandy
½ cup flour
1 pint light cream
4 egg yolks, beaten
1 teaspoon salt

Simmer lobster meat in butter until red color appears, about 15 minutes. Add other fish or shellfish. Remove pieces after they are heated through. Pour sherry and brandy over shellfish and set aside. To butter, in which lobster has been heated, add flour; make a paste. Then add cream, stirring constantly. Add a little sauce to beaten egg yolks, then combine with remainder of sauce. Add salt. Just before serving, add sea food and liquid. Do not let sauce reach boiling point after egg yolks have been added. Keep it hot in a double boiler. (Should Newburg sauce curdle, beat it with a rotary egg beater to restore smoothness.) (Makes 4 servings)

Boston Symphony Hall

POTATO KUGEL

2 pounds potatoes
1 onion
5 tablespoons chicken fat
½ teaspoon baking powder
3 eggs
1 teaspoon salt
Dash pepper

Grate or shred potatoes. Discard excess water. Grate onion into mixture. Add all other ingredients and mix well. Put 2 tablespoons of fat into mixture. Heat skillet with remaining 3 tablespoons of fat and pour mixture into skillet and bake for ¾ hour at 400°. If the kugel is browned on the bottom and top seems to be not quite done, place under broiler for a few minutes and brown on top.
(Makes 4-6 servings)
(*Traditional Jewish recipe*)

KASHA VARNISHKES

2 cups buckwheat groats
1 egg, well beaten
4 tablespoons chicken fat
1 tablespoon salt
Dash pepper
1 large onion, minced
2 stalks celery, cut in small pieces
4 cups water
1 cup egg bow noodles

Sauté the onion and celery in 2 tablespoons fat and let stand. In another frying pan, put groats in 2 tablespoons fat and add the egg. Heat and stir until the groats are thoroughly blended with the egg. Pour the boiling water into the groats, lower the flame and add the seasoning. Simmer until all water has been absorbed. Boil the egg bow noodles in plenty of water for about 20 minutes. Drain and rinse with cold water. Add egg bows and sautéed mixture to groats and bake at 350° for 15 minutes.
(Makes 4-6 servings)
(*Traditional Jewish recipe*)

Jewish Restaurant On Salem Street, circa 1895

CREAMED ONIONS

2 pounds small onions, peeled
½ cup white raisins
2 tablespoons butter
2 tablespoons flour
¼ teaspoon salt
1½ cups milk
¼ teaspoon nutmeg, ground

Cook onions in boiling salted water, covered, about 30 minutes or until tender. Drain. Simmer raisins in water to cover 10 minutes. Drain. Melt butter; add flour and salt. Add milk all at once. Cook and stir until sauce is thickened. Blend in nutmeg. Gently stir in onions and raisins. Serve hot.
(Makes 6 servings)

CREAMED FINNAN HADDIE

2 pounds finnan haddie or smoked cod
Boiling water
6 tablespoons butter or margarine
2 tablespoons onion, minced
2 tablespoons green pepper, minced
1 teaspoon paprika
6 tablespoons flour
2 cups milk
2 tablespoons pimento, minced
Parsley, chopped

Put the finnan haddie in a skillet; add just enough water to cover; simmer over low heat 10 minutes or until the fish flakes easily with a fork. Lift out the fish and drain it well. Flake it coarsely with a fork. Measure 1 cup of the fish liquid and set it aside. Melt the butter in a skillet. Add the onion and green pepper; cook over low heat, stirring occasionally, until the onion is soft but not brown. Blend in the paprika and flour. Slowly stir in the reserved fish liquid and the milk. Cook over low heat, stirring constantly, until the mixture comes to a boil. Cook and stir 3 to 5 minutes longer, until thickened. Add the fish and pimento; stir gently. Heat well. Serve garnished with chopped parsley.
(Makes 6-8 servings)

Commonwealth Avenue

CREAMED POTATOES

3 cups potatoes, cooked and diced
2 tablespoons butter, melted
1 teaspoon flour
½ teaspoon salt
½ teaspoon onion salt
1 cup light cream
Paprika

Put diced, cooked potatoes into shallow baking dish. Pour melted butter over top. Sprinkle with flour, salt and onion salt. Pour cream over mixture. Sprinkle with paprika. Bake in oven at 350° for about 30 minutes.
(Makes 4-6 servings)

HARVARD BEETS

¼ cup sugar
1 tablespoon cornstarch
¼ teaspoon salt
¼ cup beet liquid
½ cup orange juice
Grated orange rind
2 cups beets, cooked and diced or sliced
1 tablespoon butter

Mix sugar, cornstarch and salt. Add beet liquid and orange juice gradually while mixing. Add a little orange rind. Cook until thickened about 10 minutes. Add beets and butter. Combine and serve.
(Makes 4 servings)

Washington Street, Opposite Milk Street

HONEY SPICE SQUARES

1 cup honey
½ cup sugar
¾ cup shortening
2 eggs, beaten
½ cup milk
2¾ cups cake flour, sifted
1 teaspoon baking soda
1 teaspoon baking powder
1½ teaspoons salt
1 teaspoon cinnamon
¼ teaspoon cloves
¼ teaspoon nutmeg

Cream honey, sugar and shortening. Add beaten eggs. Add milk alternately with all dry ingredients, which have been sifted together. Pour into greased 8-inch square pan. Bake in oven at 325° about 25 minutes, or until done.
(Makes 12 squares)

FRUIT BARS

6 tablespoons butter or shortening
¾ cup sugar
1 egg
½ cup cooked squash
¾ cup flour, sifted
1 teaspoon baking powder
½ teaspoon salt
1 teaspoon cinnamon
¼ teaspoon nutmeg
¼ teaspoon ginger
¼ cup milk
¼ cup maraschino cherries, chopped
¼ cup raisins, plumped* and drained.

Cream butter and sugar together. Add egg and beat thoroughly. Add squash. Sift dry ingredients together. Add to creamed mixture alternately with milk. Add cherries and raisins with last of flour. Spread in greased 8-inch square pan. Bake in oven at 350° for 30 to 35 minutes.
*Add water so that raisins swell
(Makes about 18 bars)

The Old State House dates from 1748. Its outer walls, however, are older and date from 1712-1713. It has served as Town House, Court House, State House and City Hall. As the Province Court House, identified with the succession of prerevolutionary events in Boston, it has special distinction among historical buildings in the country.

State Street, Looking Towards The Old State House, Circa 1900

RHUBARB CRUMBLE PIE

2 cups fresh rhubarb
1 cup sugar
¾ cup flour, sifted
¼ cup soft butter or margarine
¼ teaspoon salt
Pastry for one 9-inch crust

Line pie plate with pastry. Combine rhubarb with ½ cup sugar and cook over medium heat until thick. Pour rhubarb filling into lined pie plate. Combine flour, butter, sugar and salt; blend well and sprinkle over filling. Bake at 375° for 35 to 40 minutes.
(Makes 6 servings)

BLUEBERRY CAKE

½ cup shortening
1 cup sugar
2 eggs
1 cup milk
2 cups flour, sifted
4 teaspoons baking powder
½ teaspoon salt
1 pint blueberries
1 cup heavy cream, whipped
Cinnamon

Cream shortening and sugar. Add eggs; beat until light. Sift flour, baking powder and salt. Add alternately with milk to creamed mixture. Fold in blueberries. Bake in 2 greased 10-inch layer cake pans in oven at 375° for about 25 minutes. Remove from oven; cool 10 minutes before turning onto cake rack. When cool, put layers together with whipped cream. Sprinkle with cinnamon.
(Makes 8 servings)

Mrs. Edward J. Lowell In Her Library, 40 Commonwealth Avenue

CABBAGE SALAD

1 medium cabbage
2 eggs
¼ teaspoon dry mustard
3 tablespoons sugar
Dash salt
¼ cup vinegar
2 tablespoons butter
½ cup heavy cream, whipped
Cayenne

Wash, drain and wipe the cabbage dry. Shred it and mix the dressing. Beat eggs slightly. Add dry ingredients and then the vinegar and butter. Put in double boiler and, stirring constantly, cook until thick. Set aside to cool. Then chill. When ready to mix with cabbage, add the whipped cream. Sprinkle with cayenne for coloring.
(makes 8-10 servings)

CHICKEN FRICASSEE

4-5 pound chicken, cut up
1 cup flour
1 teaspoon paprika
½ teaspoon salt
Dash pepper
1 quart milk
Shortening
2 tablespoons flour

Wash chicken and drain on paper towel. Mix seasonings and flour together. Dip chicken in flour mixture until well covered. Place skillet over medium heat; put in shortening and melt. Add chicken and fry until golden brown. When chicken is fried, place in casserole. Mix two tablespoons flour with ¼ cup milk. Add rest of milk and pour over chicken. Bake at 350° until chicken is tender, about 1½ hours.
(Makes 4-6 servings)

Governor's Alley, From Bromfield Street

ROAST TURKEY

10 to 12 pound turkey
Bread stuffing
Melted butter or margarine

Wash the turkey thoroughly inside and out under running water. Drain bird and pat dry. Prepare bread stuffing. Preheat oven to 325°. Fill the neck cavity of the turkey with some of the stuffing and secure the neck skin to the back with poultry pins. Fill the body cavity with stuffing and close the opening with poultry pins; lace with twine to fasten. Tie legs together; fasten to tail. Tie wings to body or fold wings under the bird. Place the bird, breast side up, on a rack in a shallow pan or open roaster. Insert a meat thermometer in the thickest part of the thigh, close to the body. Brush bird with melted butter. Roast the turkey, basting often with more melted butter or pan drippings, 4 to 4½ hours. Meat thermometer should register 190°.

BREAD STUFFING
½ cup salt pork, ground
½ cup onion, minced
⅔ cup celery, minced
2 teaspoons salt
½ teaspoon pepper
1 teaspoon poultry seasoning
8 cups bread crumbs
1 cup milk

Fry the salt pork over low heat until golden brown. Lift out pork; set aside. Stir onion and celery into the hot fat. Cook over low heat until soft but not brown. Put the onion mixture into a bowl. Add pork, salt and remaining ingredients; mix well.
(Makes 8 cups)

CRANBERRY SAUCE

4 cups cranberries
2 cups sugar
2 cups boiling water

Wash and pick over the cranberries. Combine the sugar and water in a saucepan; stir to dissolve the sugar. Bring mixture to a boil; boil 5 minutes. Add the cranberries to the boiling mixture and continue to boil without stirring until all the berries pop open. Chill before serving. (Makes 1 quart)

The S.S. Pierce Co., renowned Boston grocery store, occupied the lower floor of the Hemenway Building, built in 1884 on the site of the house where President Washington sojourned in 1789.

Four Horse Team Of Samuel S. Pierce Co., Tremont And Court Streets

INDEX

Waiting For News Of Corbett-Fitzsimmons Fight, 1897

A NOTE ON THE TYPE

The text of this book was set in a typeface called Souvenir Medium with headlines of Tiffany Heavy. Historical anecdotes were set in Souvenir Medium Italic with photograph captions in Original Script.

Boston _January 8th 1858_

Mess. Silas Pierce & Co.

To FESSENDEN & WHITTEMORE, Dr.

MANUFACTURERS, AND WHOLESALE DEALERS IN

SPICES, CREAM TARTAR, DRUGS, OAT MEAL, &c. &

No. 5, COMMERCE STREET, and CITY WHARF.

Boston Feb 27 1861

Mess. Silas Pierce & Co.

Bought of Russell, Fessenden & Whittemore,

No. 52 Chatham Street.

Bought of W. K. LEWIS & BROTHERS,

Manufacturers and Wholesale Dealers in

Ketchups, Condensed Milk, Hermetically Sealed Meats, &c.

NO. 93 BROAD STREET.

Boston Dec 27th 186

Mr. Silas Pierce & Co.

T. HAYWARD & Co., Dr.

Boston,

Mess. S. Pierce & Co.

Bought of

WHOLESALE GROCER, AND DEALE

50 & 51 CHATHAM

BOSTON AND WORCES

Entered at the Depot in Boston, by

to be forwarded by the BOSTON AND WO

to the Depot in _Worcester_

Stephen Taft Jr

ARTICLES.

One Box Sugar
Six Boxes Raisins
Two Casks Do
One Bbl Sugar
One Bbl Coffee

Boston, _Jan 10th 18 2_

Received the above for the BOSTON AND WORCESTER R

Bought of CA